Healthful Quantity Baking

Healthful Quantity Baking

Maureen Egan
Madison Area Technical College

Susan Davis Allen
Southwest Wisconsin Technical College

John Wiley & Sons, Inc.

New York · Chichester · Brisbane · Toronto · Singapore

Recognizing the importance of preserving what has been
written, it is a policy of John Wiley & Sons, Inc., to
have books of enduring value published in the United
States printed on acid-free paper, and we exert our best
efforts to that end.

The statistics, nutritional data, and other information in
this book have been obtained from many sources, including government organizations and professional health organizations. The authors and publisher have made every
reasonable effort to make this book accurate and author-
itative, but do not warrant and assume no liability for
the accuracy or completeness of the text or its fitness for
any particular purpose. The authors and publisher do not
intend for this book to be used in the treatment of medical conditions or as a substitute for professional medical
advice.

Egan, Maureen.
  Healthful quantity baking / Maureen Egan, Susan
Davis Allen.
    p.   cm.
  Includes index.
  ISBN 0-471-54022-6 (alk. paper)
  1. Baking 2. Nutrition 3. Ingredient substitutions
  (Cookery)
I. Allen, Susan Davis. II. Title.
TX763.E43   1992
641.7'1–dc20   91-15931

Printed in the United States of America

10 9 8 7 6 5 4 3 2 1

To my husband, Dave, for his expert help and encouragement,
and to our son, Jeffers, for his understanding and energy.
All my love,

Punky

To my mother, Louise Smith, who has inspired an interest in writing;
to my husband, Cecil, for sharing my work and making it easy;
to our children, Burton, Cindy, Kristy, Chris, Garrett,
and Annie for their acceptance and support.
With love and gratitude,

Susan

About the Authors

Maureen (Punky) Egan is a professional baker with over 15 years of baking experience in retail bakeries, in-store bakeries, and restaurants. She has been a baking instructor at Madison Area Technical College for the past six years. A coauthor of two low-fat, low-calorie dessert cookbooks, she currently writes a monthly column on healthful baking for *Bakery Production and Marketing*.

Susan Davis Allen is a registered dietitian with bachelor's and master's degrees from Montana State University. She has taken additional graduate coursework at Kansas State University and the University of Wisconsin. She is currently on the staff of Southwest Wisconsin Technical College as a nutrition specialist and instructor and is the consulting dietitian for the University of Wisconsin-Platteville. She has had 10 years of experience writing and publishing five nutrition education curricula and has published in the *Journal of Nutrition Education* and the *School Food Service Review*. In addition, she has had 15 years of experience teaching in the area of food science and nutrition. Baking has always been a hobby, and she has enjoyed reformulating recipes to offer friends and family healthier versions of old favorites.

PREFACE

The American public's concern for health and physical well-being has brought about changes in the food service industries. Grocers now stock leaner meats and low-fat dairy items, along with sugar- and salt-free products. Restaurants, likewise, offer their customers expanded salad bars and lower-calorie entrees. Currently, the baking industry is looking at ways to produce healthier products. The purpose of this book is to promote healthy and delicious alternatives to traditional "made-from-scratch" baked products without utilizing expensive fat and sugar substitutes or other artificial ingredients.

This book seeks to answer current questions about nutrition as it relates to baking. We believe that it will serve as (1) a supplemental textbook that provides students enrolled in quantity baking courses with solid theoretical and practical information about healthful baking practices; (2) an easy-to-use, accurate nutrition resource for bakers interested in expanding their market; and (3) a source of tasty recipes that have been tested and that meet the demands of today's health-conscious consumer.

ORGANIZATION

A significant portion of the population has become motivated enough to accept nutrition as an important standard for their food choices. How can the baking industry better understand the nutritional marketplace and produce healthier baked goods for its customers? This book is structured to guide the reader along the path to that answer.

Healthful Quantity Baking is divided into two parts. In Part I, Chapter 1 reviews the historical use of bakery ingredients. The second chapter examines food choices and how and why they are changing.

Chapter 3 presents the nutritional aspects of baking, exploring the ingredients used in baking and their nutritional significance. Chapter 4 studies current nutritional recommendations of the U. S. government and various health organizations.

The fifth chapter looks closely at nutritional labeling language and proposals for changes in that language. Chapter 6 investigates healthful baking ingredients and their application to Part II.

Part II contains healthful recipes, many of which are classic desserts and pastries. However, we have reformulated them for lower fat, lower sugar, lower sodium, and higher fiber content.

To supplement and enhance the text, we have included many illustrations and tables to help the reader grasp the theoretical and practical ideas being presented. The question marks in the margins of Chapter 3 draw attention to dietary concerns that are answered in the adjacent text. Each recipe, or formula, includes nutritional information calculated using the software program Food Processor II from ESHA of Salem, Oregon. Finally, appendices identify the nutritional benefits of each recipe and the proposed labeling standards; a glossary defines new or technical terms.

ACKNOWLEDGMENTS

We wish to thank the following individuals for their professional critique of and suggestions for the text; for testing and retesting the formulas; and for their expertise as tasters: from the Southwest Wisconsin Technical College, Gayle Antony, Ronald Coppernoll, Harriet Copus, Sue Medeke, Jolly Michel, Al Probst, Dr. Richard Rogers; from the University of Wisconsin-Platteville Bakery, Deborah Putnam, Jackie Retallick; Gary Engelke, Hometown Bakery, Platteville, WI; Eunice Bassler, Iowa State University; Pat Shemek, Castle Rock Catering, Castle Rock, WI; Louise Smith, Seattle, WA; from the Madison Area Technical College, Mary Hill, Jean Hammen, Robert Hurst, James Freese; Diane Lefebvre, Dan Egan, and Penny Ballantyne, Madison, WI; and Carol Meres Kroskey, *Bakery Production and Marketing*.

Special thanks to Burton Davis for his computer graphics and to our editor, Claire Thompson, at John Wiley & Sons.

CONTENTS

Healthful Quantity Baking

PART
I

BAKING AND NUTRITION

1 BAKING INGREDIENTS A BRIEF HISTORY

Food ingredients of all kinds have changed markedly over time with the development of international trading and technological advance. In this chapter, we will review the history of baking and the three main ingredients of baked goods: wheat, sugar and fats.

Between 3500 and 3000 B.C., the Egyptians discovered—perhaps serendipitously—the fermentation process, and leavened bread making soon became a widely practiced craft. By combining wheat flour with different grains and other ingredients, Egyptians were able to bake over fifty different types of breads. The peoples of the Mediterranean area gradually obtained the knowledge of baking leavened bread from the Egyptians and contributed their own expertise to the baking process, including more sophisticated milling techniques, better ovens, and written records of their processes. They quickly expanded bread and cake recipes to include eggs, nuts, and a variety of herbs and spices. Wheat, however, remained the preferred grain in all of these products.

Until the mid-1800s, sugar was a luxury item; as a bakery ingredient, it was used only in speciality confections. Since then it has become cheaper, more plentiful, and more widely used. Today, per-person sugar consumption is at an all-time high level.

Humans have used fats, such as olive oil and butter, since ancient times both as a food and for other purposes, including hair and body ointments, and for tool lubricants. To meet the demand for a cheaper butter substitute, margarine was invented, and all-vegetable shortenings soon followed. Because of these plentiful, low-cost substitutions, our per capita consumption of total fats has also increased every year.

Some of the ingredient choices for bakery products were obviously made on economic grounds. Some were based on technological abilities.

Still others were influenced by the fashion of an era. An examination of a few basic baking ingredients will promote an understanding of their sources and the ways in which they achieved a fixed place in today's baking.

THE MILLING OF WHEAT

Grains were one of the first crops that humans domesticated; barley and wheat were cultivated around 7000 B.C. Through the ages most cultures have consumed a carbohydrate-rich diet based on grains and supplemented with vegetables and meat. Some cultures continue to serve these traditional grain dishes and obtain a substantial amount of their nutrients from these foods.

Humans probably first ate grains as a porridge or gruel, cooking the grains until soft and edible. Somewhat later, this gruel may have been spread onto hot stones and cooked, forming a crude, flat sheet. These first flat breads were probably very tough and coarse. A logical next step was to crush the grain—probably wheat—in order to shorten the cooking time and give the bread a lighter texture.

One of the first milling implements was a cuplike vessel, most likely a hollowed-out stone that held the grain, with a pestle like stone ball to crush the grain into a coarse meal. A variation of this type of grinding tool evolved in Egypt around 3500 B.C. Known as the saddlestone, it consisted of a slightly concave bottom stone that held the grain and an oblong roller stone used to pulverize the grain. This early type of mill was used in most households. Despite the Egyptian discovery of fermentation, their flour, and subsequently their breads, were relatively coarse, owing to the crude milling on the saddlestones. Although this process was adequate for the household, many years passed before any significant developments occurred in milling on a larger, more refined scale.

The first continuous rotary hourglass and quern mills were developed around 300 B.C. These mills had a rotating top stone that also acted as a hopper, feeding the grain into a narrow horizontal space between it and a stationary bottom stone. Animals or humans propelled the top stone by pushing on wooden handles that extended from it, thereby grinding the grain. Smaller versions, known as quern mills, were used in households. Sifting, or bolting, of the flour began during this period in an effort to remove some of the bran and any foreign particles that may have gotten into the wheat. This extra procedure produced the relatively white flour that the nobility so highly prized.

The next breakthroughs came as societies began to capture the mechanical energy of water, and later wind, to power grain mills. Water mills first appeared in Greece around 200 B.C. These vertical-shaft water mills liberated young women from the drudgery of operating the old-fashioned querns. This design later became known in other parts of Europe and in China and Japan. The Roman architect and engineer Vitruvius first described a horizontal-shaft water mill about 27 B.C. This design spread throughout the Roman Empire and continued to be used in Europe until the early ninteenth century (see Figure 1.1).

Windmills have a history similar to that of water mills, although their use began somewhat later. The earliest known references to wind-driven grain mills come from ninth-century Arabic writings that describe a 644 A.D. windmill in Persia. European contact with the Arabic world during

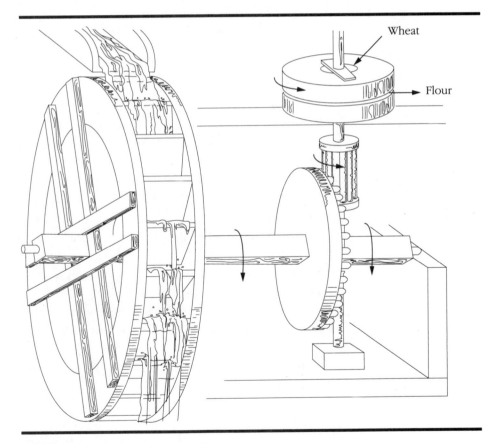

FIGURE 1.1
A water wheel

the Crusades helped them acquire the technology necessary to develop the now-familiar vertical-sailed windmill.

These water mills and windmills greatly expanded the capacity to mill grain. They produced more horsepower than earlier methods and could therefore drive large millstones, or *burrstones*. Thus, more flour could be produced to support expanding European populations.

Even with the watermills and windmills, the resulting white flour was very different from the white flour of today. The relatively slow grinding of the wheat between the burrstones crushed the wheat grain, causing the oil from the germ to permeate the flour. It also caused parts of the bran to become so finely ground that they would not sift out, giving the flour a speckled appearance.

From the 1300s to the 1700s, the sifting process consisted of putting the flour first through a net or sieve to remove the coarsest particles, and then through a woolen bolting cloth. The resulting flour, the finest white flour of its day, still contained small amounts of bran and wheat germ, along with pulverized bits of stone from the millstones. In the mid-eighteenth century, a much finer silk gauze bolting cloth replaced the woolen one, resulting in a whiter flour because less bran was able to pass through the closely woven silk material.

Wheat cultivation and milling in the United States during the early 1800s emulated the European process. Millers chose sites along rivers to make use of the water power and for transportation purposes. Later in the century, with the onset of the Industrial Revolution, mills became steam-powered.

At the same time, a revolutionary new system of milling was developed in Switzerland that drastically changed the milling operation. To grind the wheat, this new mill incorporated a series of high-speed metal and porcelain rollers that completely separated the germ and bran from the endosperm. The process also incorporated a purifier system that used a blast of air to remove the bran.

Teamed with the newly invented steam engine, the roller mills could grind substantially more flour than either the windmill or watermill. The resulting flour was also much whiter in color, owing to the complete separation of the bran and germ. This type of mill, known as a roller mill, rapidly became the standard for wheat milling operations, completely replacing the old burrstones.

Today, flour milling is even more sophisticated than it was a hundred years ago. Many extractions of flour are now available. In fact, all white flours are so refined that the milling process now removes 14 vitamins and minerals either completely or partially and all of the bran. Since the 1940s, the U.S. government has required mills to enrich their white flour by adding four vitamins: iron, thiamin, riboflavin, and niacin.

SUGAR

Sucrose, the ingredient we know as table sugar, is a relatively new food to most peoples of the world. Even though humans first cultivated sugar cane in New Guinea around 8000 B.C., it did not achieve a permanent place in our daily diets until the late 1800s. The reasons for its rise stem from a variety of causes ranging from the appeal of its natural sweetness to some significant economic and social factors.

Methods of growing sugar cane and techniques for extracting sugar gradually spread from New Guinea and the East Indies to India two thousand years ago, and continued westward to the southern and eastern shores of the Mediterranean. Sugar eventually found its way to the tables of European royalty when knights returned from the Crusades in the twelfth century with this sweet and rare substance. Throughout the Middle Ages in Europe, sugar was scarce and available at a price only the wealthy and powerful could afford.

About 1100 A.D., merchants began to bring spices, including sugar, from the East into Europe. At the time, sugar was grouped with pepper, nutmeg, cardamom, coriander, and other exotic spices as an expensive flavor additive. Wealthy Europeans used sugar as a spice to enhance the flavor of their food rather than as a sweetener.

Sugar also became widely used as a medicinal aid. All around the Mediterranean, sugar has a long history as a remedy for a variety of illnesses, including fever, dry coughs, and stomach diseases, to name a few. This unique use of sugar was introduced into continental Europe probably through Italy by way of Arab pharmacology. By the sixteenth century, this use of sugar was widespread. Not every physician, however, was convinced of sugar's healing properties, and lively debates regarding its medicinal benefits continued for centuries. Sugar gradually lost this medicinal function only after it became plentiful and consumed in large amounts (although to this day, medicine is sweetened to make it more palatable).

An interesting, and unique, use of sugar is as a decorative medium. The craft evolved from the splendid sugarwork of the Middle East and Africa. Bakers there constructed elaborate displays, including animal figures, structures, and other objects with a claylike dough made from sugar, oil, crushed nuts, and vegetable gums. These impressive centerpieces were also edible and were usually consumed at the

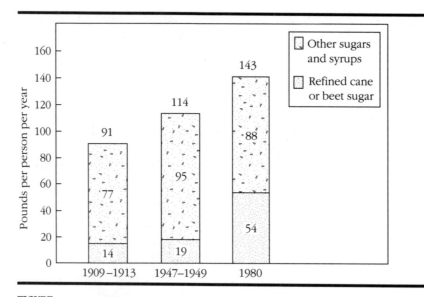

FIGURE 1.2

Total yearly U.S. sugar consumption from 1909 to 1980 (adapted from the
USDA Economic Research Service)

end of the feast. French bakers had begun casting sugar into marzipan
figures for royal feasts by the thirteenth century. Other European
countries quickly adapted this new art form. To this day, many bakers
continue this traditional art.

In 1747, the process for extracting sugar from the juice of the white beet
was perfected in France. Continental Europe then had a steady supply of
sugar within its borders. By the late nineteenth century, sugar had become
a necessity in both Europe and the United States.

Per capita consumption of all sugars (cane, beet, and corn) in the United
States has risen steadily from a low of 2 pounds per year in 1700 to over
140 pounds by 1980. There has been a slight decrease in cane and beet sugar
usage, but with the rapid rise of corn sweeteners, mainly in beverages, sugar
consumption continues to increase (see Figure 1.2).

FATS

The human body needs some fats to perform essential bodily functions. It
is therefore not surprising that fats have played an important role in the
human diet for millennia. Historically, cultures have always incorporated
some type of fat, depending on their location, into their diets.

For instance, the peoples in the Mediterranean area have considered olive oil an important element in their diets and in their lives for thousands of years. They used the oil not only for food, but for other purposes as well. The Egyptians used it as a lubricant for moving heavy building materials. It was also used for making candles and lamps. In religious ceremonies, olive oil made the principal anointing agent. As a beauty aid, olive oil made an excellent base for perfumes and soaps as well as for body lotions and hair dressings.

Butter was an often-used fat from ancient times in other parts of the world, including northern and central Europe. Cultures that maintained cattle herds had easy access to the many products of milk, including cheese, yogurt, and butter. Butter was used for many of the same purposes as olive oil—namely, as food, in religious ceremonies, as a lubricant, and in beauty products.

Both olive oil and butter were highly prized for the unique properties that made them an integral part of the societies that used them. However, both were problematic. Olive oil was difficult to produce and, like butter, hard to preserve and transport very far from the production source. These shortcomings, especially in the case of butter, led to a search for a cheaper and more plentiful butter substitute.

Margarine was invented in 1869 by a French chemist, H. Mege Mouries, who used suet and milk as his main ingredients. By the late 1800s, margarine production was well under way in the United States. A new development occurred around the turn of the century, when a method for hardening oil was discovered and perfected. After discovering that animal fats remained solid at room temperature because they were saturated with hydrogen molecules, researchers found they could also harden liquid oils by adding hydrogen to them. Because of many processes involved in hydrogenation, including bleaching and deodorizing the oil, it made no difference which plant was used for the source of the oil. The cheapest plant source was the one used, and the public could finally indulge in a cheap butter substitute. During the early 1900s in the United States, this technique was used with cottonseed oil, an abundant by-product of the cotton industry of the South, to produce the first hydrogenated shortening. The use of domestic oils helped eliminate federal and state restrictions against the use of margarine.

Consumption of different fats has fluctuated over the years, but, unfortunately, the overall consumption for total fats has steadily increased to a current all-time high of over 60 pounds per person per year. (See Figure 1.3). In fact, approximately 40 percent of the calories consumed in the United States come from fat.

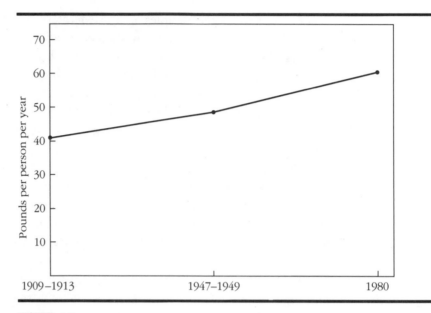

FIGURE 1.3
Total yearly U.S. fat consumption from 1909 to 1980 (adapted from the USDA Economic Research Service)

BIBLIOGRAPHY

Cabe, Carl. *Flour Milling.* Kansas Industry Series No. 2. Lawrence, KS: School of Business—Bureau of Business Research, University of Kansas, 1958.

Jacob, H. E. *Six Thousand Years of Bread.* Translated by Richard Winston and Clara Winston. Garden City, New York: Doubleday, Doran and Company, Inc., 1944.

Mintz, Sidney W. *Sweetness and Power.* New York: Elisabeth Sifton Books, Viking Penguin, 1985.

Sheppard, Ronald, and Edward Newton. *The Story of Bread.* London: Routledge and Kegan Paul, 1957.

Visser, Margaret. *Much Depends on Dinner.* New York, New York: Grove Press, 1986.

ACTIVITY

Much of the fat and sugar we eat is hidden within processed foods, such as bakery products, frozen dinners, canned soups, and condiments. These are called "invisible" sugars and fats. We may not even realize that we are eating fat and sugar when we consume these products, much less know the amounts of them. "Visible" fats and sugars are those we add ourselves when preparing foods, so we have control over the amounts we use.

Use the following table to keep track of the types of foods containing "visible" and "invisible" sugars and fats you eat in a week. Read food labels carefully to find all the sources. For example, sugar can also be listed as corn syrup, dextrose, honey, and the like. Is more of your intake of fats and sugars taken in the recognizable, visible form—table sugar, honey, oil, margarine, and such—or in the disguised, invisible form? An example of each category is shown in the following table.

DAY	INVISIBLE SUGAR	INVISIBLE FAT	VISIBLE SUGAR	VISIBLE FAT
example	*bakery rye bread*	*frozen pizza*	*sugar on cereal*	*oil on salad*
Sunday				
Monday				
Tuesday				
Wednesday				
Thursday				
Friday				
Saturday				

2 FOOD CHOICES

FACTORS INFLUENCING FOOD SELECTION

As nutritional research continues to indicate a strong correlation between diet and good health, the adage "You are what you eat" rings anew with intensity and vigor. But there is more to making food choices than a knowledge of nutrition; therefore, understanding how such decisions are made requires a multidimensional approach. In this chapter we will explore the factors that individuals and society use to shape their food selections.

To say that numerous factors constitute the realm of our food choices is an understatement. In fact, researchers have conservatively enumerated 16 general categories related to stable food preferences—-food characteristics, age, family relations, television, culture, self-concept, socioeconomic status, sex, peer pressure, body weight, race, food familiarity, nutritional knowledge, parental attitudes, food associations, and geography (see Lyman, *A Psychology of Food*). These factors do not act separately but interact with one another to produce, over space and time, the world of human food choices. Consequently, making food choices implies more than simply eating whatever "tastes good." Yet many people, including those who make the food, never consider this aspect of their daily lives.

It is important to understand that this process does exist and to explore what it means. Figure 2.1—a generalized model of the process—focuses attention on food availability as well as the social, psychological, cost, and nutritional factors leading to food choice.

AVAILABILITY

Food availability plays a fundamental role in determining our food choices because you can eat only the food you have at hand. For example, people

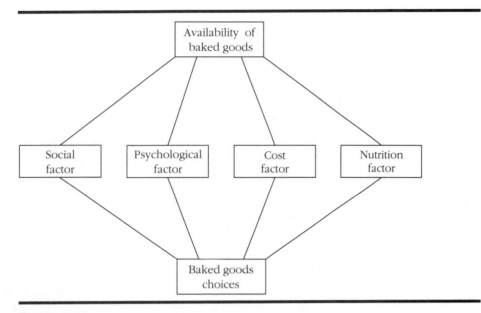

FIGURE 2.1
Factors influencing choices of baked goods

who recall the food rationing and "victory gardens" in the United States during World Wars I and II can realize how diets and recipes become altered by availability. On the other hand, no culture eats every edible food available to it. For example, insects might be considered a delicacy by an Indonesian but not by an American.

Until five hundred years ago, most humans grew, gathered, hunted, or traded their foods principally within a regionally defined area. With the advent of expanded sea trade by European nations in the late fifteenth century, a new chapter in human history began, bringing a greater variety of food ingredients to countries actively involved in trade and colonization. Before this exploration, Europe was limited in its choices to locally grown foods, except for rare and expensive Asian spices imported to Venice through the Middle East. By the seventeenth century, as non-European areas became colonized with settlers and plantations, different commodities, including spices, sugar, tea, coffee, and chocolate, became more readily available to Europeans. These foods were soon assimilated into their diet.

Today, in the United States and throughout the industrialized world, there is a tremendous variety of foods available from around the globe. With so many foods available, there must be other factors that explain why we choose one food over another.

THE SOCIAL FACTOR

As Lyman's list of the 16 food choice factors suggests, a society's influence on individual food choice has multiple aspects.

One of the strongest social relations with food exists because people have historically shared food among themselves, thereby creating a common bond by the food they ate together. This social norm has persevered through the ages; and, whether eating is formal or informal, it always has a measure of ritual embedded within it. This fulfills a social need, a need we are loathe to break. Thus we are prone to eat the same kinds of food our friends and neighbors eat. Even today, when it seems we have lost our sense of community, we still tend to share similar dietary habits because food choices are firmly rooted in our culture and typically change very slowly, unless heavily influenced by the media.

Another social influence is one's socioeconomic status. For example, white flour, although rarer and more expensive, has been available to the privileged class since baking began. By selecting these rare foods, the nobles set themselves apart from the peasants, using food as one symbol of their prestige. Later, when these foods became more plentiful and cheaper, the less privileged population emulated the wealthy by choosing the same foods and incorporating them into their diets. Even today, food maintains its role as a status symbol, as evidenced by the wide array of foods for banquets, parties, and other social gatherings found at various levels of sophistication throughout society.

One unfortunate social influence on food choice in society today is the perverse use of food to achieve a particular body shape. The perception of slimness as an ideal has led to a variety of eating disorders in some populations. A negative self-concept, shaped by social forces, may cause some individuals to make food choices that are detrimental to good health.

THE PSYCHOLOGICAL FACTOR

Another factor affecting food choice results from our psychological perception of different foods. Two important aspects of this factor are familiarity and food associations. We tend to eat foods similar to those we ate as children simply because they are familiar. This is not to say that humans cannot find new foods pleasurable but rather that some learning and sense of adventure are required to do so. We also associate different foods with different sensations and experiences. Naturally, unpleasant experiences make us avoid foods with which they are connected, while the opposite is true for pleasant experiences. Moreover, all foods have characteristic flavors, textures, and, most importantly, odors that we associate with and expect of them. Peanut butter cookies, for example, smell and taste like peanut butter and have a firm, crunchy texture. Anything offered as a substitute that does not have these characteristics would be rejected as unauthentic. When considering substitutes for "old favorites," then, a baker should be aware that these associations must be maintained in order to achieve an acceptable alternative.

Food is such a common aspect of our lives that we use it to reward and punish not only ourselves but others as well. An extra-rich dessert to reward an accomplishment is typically counterbalanced by food deprivation because of some misbehavior. And, of course, eating foods we find comforting can help relieve tension and calm us.

COST AND CONVENIENCE

Cost and convenience also influence food choices. At one time or another, many people find themselves facing tight budgets. During those times, they tend to purchase foods that are bargain-priced or give them the best perceived value. For example, we might spend more than our budget allows for a special meal on an occasion like a birthday. On the other hand, we often purchase items because of their lower price, regardless of any other factor.

Today, as more people work outside the home, less time is available for other activities, including food preparation. Convenience, therefore, becomes yet another factor in food selection. This is true especially where disposable income is high and available time for food preparation short. Individuals or families in these situations typically purchase convenience foods with their additional income, as shown in recent decades by the emergence and growth of fast-food chains and the decline of food preparation in the home.

THE NUTRITIONAL FACTOR

The nutritional link between food and health has various precedents—for example, the use of certain plants or animal parts to restore health or avoid illness in medieval times, or the work of Dr. John Kellogg of Michigan, who developed various nut and vegetable products for his patients during the last decades of the nineteenth century. An acceptance of this relationship developed as the science of nutrition matured during this century.

In recent years, however, this knowledge has become especially focused in the hearts and minds of the general public because of an increasing emphasis on physical fitness; a national concern for personal health due to the rise in diet-related diseases, namely, heart attacks and various types of cancer; and a heightened awareness about the potential danger of chemical or "unnatural" additives in foods. One pertinent example of a population that has reordered its diet is survivors of heart attacks. They must now eat low-salt, low-fat, and generally healthier foods that will allow them to live a longer, more active life.

This emphasis on health remains strong and suggests that more and more consumers will base their food choices not only on familiarity and convenience, but on nutritional value as well.

HEALTHFUL BAKERY CHOICES

A variety of factors act together to affect food choices. With the growing amount of data showing that foods affect our health, we should carefully consider the nutritional value of the foods we consume. The deadly diseases of today are diseases of excesses. Remember, the choice is ours. The more we know about the reasons behind our selections, the better we can make intelligent food choices.

In our baking, we need to consider the nutritional value of ingredients as valid a concern as any other factor. We should restructure our recipes to use ingredients that meet basic nutritional standards. Only then will consumers have a complete array of healthful bakery choices.

BIBLIOGRAPHY

Ilmonen, K. Food Choices in Modern Society. In *Nutritional Adaptation to New Life-Styles*. Edited by J. C. Somogyi and E. H. Koskinen. Basel, Switzerland: Buchdruckerei Basler Zeitung, 1990.

Levenstein, Harvey A. *Revolution at the Table*. New York: Oxford University Press, 1988.

Lyman, Bernard. *A Psychology of Food*. New York: Van Nostrand Reinhold, 1989.

Mennell, Steven. *All Manners of Food*. Oxford, England: Basil Blackwell Ltd., 1985.

Mueller, H.R. Nutritional Adaption to New Life-Styles: Conclusions. In *Nutritional Adaptation to New Life-Styles*. Edited by J. C. Somogyi and E. H. Koskinen. Basel, Switzerland: Buchdruckerei Basler Zeitung, 1990.

ACTIVITY

Keep track of any bakery foods you eat tomorrow. What factors influenced your choices? Record the foods and your reasons as shown below. Compare the reasons for your choices with those outlined in this chapter.

Examples:

Social factor *Had birthday cake with family members.*

Psychological factor *Aced a test, so treated myself to a rich dessert.*

Cost factor *Bought cookies because they were on sale.*

Nutrition factor *Ate a bagel instead of a sweet roll for breakfast.*

Social factor

Psychological factor

Cost factor

Nutrition factor

3

NUTRITION
ITS RELATIONSHIP TO BAKING

Science can be defined as the knowledge one gains through study or continual practice. The study and practice of combining baking ingredients into a finished product comprise the science of baking. Other contributing factors are the chemical reactions taking place during the baking process and the formulas (recipes) you follow.

Nutrition is the study of the nutrient needs of the body and the combining of these nutrients for optimal health. *Healthful baking* is the combination of the sciences of baking and nutrition. Ingredients are combined to produce a finished product that will meet the criteria of taste and nutrition. Some basic nutrition principles are helpful in understanding healthy baking.

Nutrients are substances in foods that, when properly combined, provide optimum health. These food components supply our bodies with energy, promote the growth and maintenance of tissues, and regulate body processes. There are approximately 50 known nutrients that can be divided into six categories: carbohydrates, proteins, fats, vitamins, minerals, and water. The first three provide energy, the amount of which is expressed in Calories:

Protein provides 4 Calories per gram.

Carbohydrate provides 4 Calories per gram.

Fat provides 9 Calories per gram.

The other three categories of nutrients—vitamins, minerals, and water—do not provide Calories (and therefore provide no energy). They function by helping to release energy from food and assist the energy nutrients in the growth, maintenance, and regulation of body tissues and life processes (see Figure 3.1).

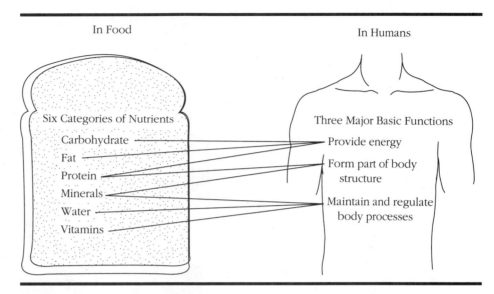

FIGURE 3.1
Nutrients and their functions

THE ENERGY NUTRIENTS

CARBOHYDRATES

Carbohydrates are called *simple* if they are sugars, or *complex* if they are starches or fiber. They are the major source of energy in our diet. Over half of our daily calories should come from carbohydrates, particularly starches. Knowledge of carbohydrates begins with definition of relevant vocabulary.

The word *saccharide* means sugar; the number of molecules of sugar linked together determines the class of carbohydrate. For instance, a monosaccharide is a carbohydrate containing one sugar molecule. You can think of it as a single chain link. Carbohydrates known as simple sugars are either mono- or disaccharides (one or two sugar links). Complex carbohydrates usually contain many monosaccharide links and are known as polysaccharides. Two other categories of carbohydrates are alcohol sugars and alcohol. As components of food, these mono-, di-, and polysaccharides have more common names. Figure 3.2 lists the common names and food sources of these carbohydrates.

CARBOHYDRATES IN DIGESTION

Carbohydrates are the most readily absorbed of the energy nutrients. The body breaks down both simple and complex carbohydrates to the simple sugar glucose. To resolve the controversy over sugar versus honey: both

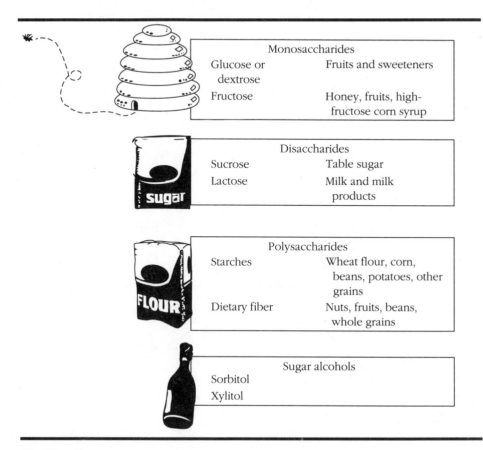

FIGURE 3.2
Common names and food sources of carbohydrates

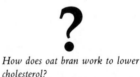

Is honey better for you than sugar?

How does oat bran work to lower cholesterol?

are broken down to glucose, so the end result of digestion is the same. Glucose is the preferred energy source for operating the brain and nervous system, and for performing physical activity and basic body functions. The liver and muscles store excess glucose as a polysaccharide called *glycogen*. When those stores are full, glycogen is stored as body fat. People who have such medical problems as lactose intolerance, hypoglycemia, or diabetes have trouble properly digesting carbohydrates and may be on special diets.

Complex carbohydrates in the form of oat or rice bran have recently made the news. Oat bran represents one of two types of dietary fiber. It is a *soluble* fiber that, combined with water, forms a gel. Some of the gel-forming carbohydrates have been found to decrease the absorption of cholesterol. The second type of fiber is *insoluble*. Examples of this type are wheat bran, barley, and seeds. Insoluble fiber increases the movement of food through the digestive tract. Humans need both types of dietary fiber for proper nutrition and digestion.

CARBOHYDRATES IN BAKING

In baking, carbohydrates are categorized as sweeteners (simple sugars), thickeners (starches), or bulking agents (fiber). There are now more than 100 sweet substances called sugars. Processed products contain most of the sugar consumed in the United States. As you begin to understand carbohydrates in baking, you will recognize these sweeteners as carbohydrates, which contribute four Calories per gram to the daily diet. For example, a recipe for six dozen cookies calls for 10 oz of sugar. This is about 4 g of sugar per cookie or 16 Calories from sugar. Sugars, as noted in Figure 3.2, frequently end in -*ose* and sugar alcohols end in -*ol*. You can immediately see that the ingredient dextr*ose* is a sugar, and sorbit*ol* is a sugar alcohol. When these sweeteners are added to a baked product, the product contains a mono- or disaccharide that breaks down during digestion to the simple sugar glucose. Sugar alcohols are chemically similar to sugar and contribute four Calories per gram. Bakers should not be fooled into using a sugar alcohol as a sweetener to reduce Calories. In fact, artificially sweetened products may not help your customers control their weight.

Can using sugar alcohols help me lose weight?

What is invert sugar?

Sweeteners come in different forms, from powdered and crystalline to syrup. Table sugar is a disaccharide—sucrose—that usually comes in crystalline form. Powdered sugar, or confectioners' sugar, is table sugar ground to a fine powder. Brown sugar is table sugar containing a small amount of molasses. Honey, molasses, and, of course, corn syrup are syrups. Invert sugar is a syrup commonly used in the baking industry; it is produced by chemically changing the disaccharide sucrose into a syrup comprised of the monosaccharides fructose and glucose. Monosaccharides usually taste sweeter than polysaccharides, so less invert sugar, honey, or high-fructose corn syrup is needed to produce the same sweetness as sucrose. When less sweetener is used, the product contains fewer calories.

Until about 1970, most of the sweeteners used in baking came from processing sugarcane or sugar beets. However, with the advent of high-fructose corn syrup—a derivative of processed corn—the preferred sweetener has shifted from mainly cane or beet sugar to corn sweetener. Today, a crystalline fructose, processed from high-fructose corn syrup, is also available. Whatever the sweetener of choice in the baking industry is, you should keep in mind that "sucrose-free" does not mean "sugar-free." All sweeteners, except for those classified as artificial, contain four Calories per gram and are metabolized in the body to glucose. Some of the new artificial sweeteners are nutritive and also provide four Calories per gram. Chapter 6 reviews these products. Since one of the purposes of this book is to promote reducing the total amount of sugar, rather than substituting, we will not discuss the non-nutritive artificial sweeteners such as saccharin or cyclamates.

Thickeners (starches) and bulking agents (fiber) are also carbohydrates containing four Calories per gram. Foods made from grains are ONE of the main sources of starch. Wheat flour is the most commonly used starch in baking. Others include rye flour, oatmeal, cornmeal, cornstarch, and, in some areas of the country, triticale flour (a hybrid grain of wheat and rye). Whole wheat flour, graham flour, wheat and rice bran, and stoneground cornmeal contain insoluble fiber, while oatmeal, oat bran, apples, and citrus fruits provide soluble fiber. These two types of fiber behave differently in baking.

PROTEINS

Like carbohydrates, protein provides four Calories per gram. However, unlike carbohydrates, protein is rarely found by itself; it is usually found in combination with fat. The word *protein* comes from a Greek word meaning "of prime importance." Protein has been considered to be "of prime importance" for decades. However, most people now eat too much protein, resulting in a diet also higher in fat.

To understand the importance of protein, you should review Figure 3.1. One can see that protein is responsible for the growth and maintenance of tissues. In fact, protein is found in all body tissues. It is made up of smaller units called *amino acids*. Protein is rated according to the amounts and types of amino acids it contains. A good-quality protein contains all the essential amino acids; *essential* is defined as those amino acids the body cannot make and must therefore be derived from foods. Foods containing all the essential amino acids are also referred to as *complete proteins*. Examples of complete proteins can be found in Figure 3.3.

Meat Products

Beef
Pork
Lamb
Poultry
Fish

Dairy Products

Milk
Cheese

Eggs

FIGURE 3.3
Examples of complete proteins

?

Can "man" live by bread alone?

Incomplete proteins are those lacking either the amount or the type of amino acid needed for growth and maintenance of tissues. These lower-quality proteins are the ones found in bakery products such as breads, grains, cereals or nuts. Legumes also contain lower-quality protein. Figure 3.4 shows incomplete protein foods that, when combined, will supply the essential amino acids. The body's need for the essential amino acids found in complete proteins can also be met through a variety of plant foods consumed on a daily basis. You could also increase the quality of an incomplete protein by combining it with a complete protein such as milk or eggs.

PROTEIN IN DIGESTION

The body cannot store proteins. After a protein food is eaten, it is broken down into amino acids. Proteins are absorbed and carried to the cells to be used for growth and maintenance. If extra protein is consumed, it is further broken down and either used for energy, if needed, or stored as fat. Can you see the danger of eating too much protein?

PROTEINS IN BAKING

When protein foods are heated, a change called *denaturation* occurs in their molecular shape. *Coagulation* is one form of denaturation that occurs when cooking, for example, an egg or egg custard. Gluten, the protein in flour, also coagulates when heated, forming the structure desired in breads.

Flours contain a small amount of protein, but the amount of protein affects the quality of the finished baked product. Therefore, flours are categorized according to their protein content. High-protein flours are called

Legumes + Grains

Dried beans + rice
Dried peas + corn
Dried beans + corn

Grains + Nuts

Peanut butter + bread

Soy Products + Seeds

Soybeans + sesame seeds
Tofu + sunflower seeds

FIGURE 3.4
Incomplete protein combinations

high-gluten flour, or *bread flour.* Cake flour and cornstarch are much lower in protein, as is rye flour. Because gluten—protein—helps give structure to bread, breads made with high-gluten flour have a much greater volume than breads made with cake flour or rye flour. Flours are sources of incomplete proteins, whereas eggs and milk are sources of complete proteins used in baking. Fruit and vegetables contain only small amounts of incomplete protein. The soybean is an exception. When it is milled into soy meal, it contains almost 50 percent protein. Isolated soy protein and casein or whey, isolated from cow's milk, are protein foods more recently found in the bakery.

FAT

Currently, fats are the most confusing and most discussed nutrient used in baking. They are an integral part of our diet, adding flavor, some nutrients, and an appealing texture. They contribute more than twice as many Calories per gram as carbohydrate or protein. There are also many different forms of fat available, and they yield different finished products. Some of these forms are associated with chronic diseases. Therefore, the finished product's taste and general quality as well as its health factors should be considered when you choose a fat for a baked product.

How do you choose the "right" fat? Clarifying some fat facts and fallacies will help answer this question. The chemical term for fats in general is *lipid.* The most common lipid is a *triglyceride,* which represents about 95 percent of the lipids in our food. A triglyceride is composed of three (tri-) glycerol (glyceride) units to which a fatty acid is attached. You may be familiar with the term *fatty acid* from hearing the words "saturated fatty acid," "monounsaturated fatty acid," and "polyunsaturated fatty acid." A saturated fatty acid, as the word *saturated* implies, is the fatty acid with the greatest concentration of hydrogen atoms; it is *saturated* with them. A saturated fat is usually solid at room temperature. Examples of saturated fats are butter, lard, fat in and around meat, and coconut and palm oils. Semihard fats, such as margarines containing corn oil, as well as olive and canola (or rapeseed) oils, are considered monounsaturated fats. Monounsaturated fats are less concentrated with hydrogen. Other oils such as soybean, sesame, corn, and safflower are polyunsaturated fats. Polyunsaturated fats, as one might guess, have the smallest concentration of hydrogen.

Some of the unsaturated fats like corn oil may be made more concentrated by a process called *hydrogenation,* during which more hydrogen is added to the fatty acid. A hydrogenated fat—vegetable shortening, for example—is chemically more like a saturated fat. Food sources of the three types of fatty acids used in baking are found in Figure 3.5. An important fact to remember here is whether the fat is saturated, monosaturated, or polyunsaturated, it still contains 9 Calories per gram.

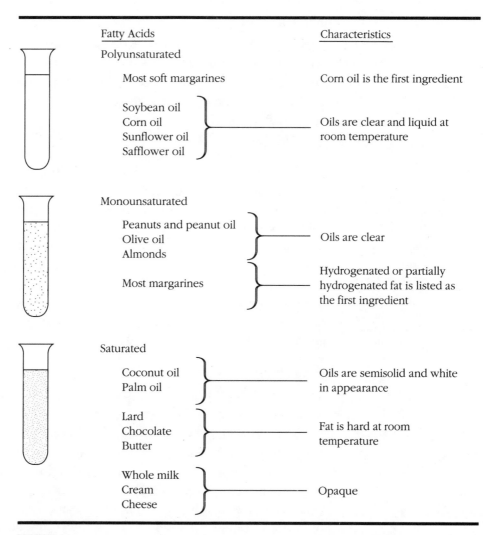

FIGURE 3.5
Characteristics of fatty acids used in baking

The second type of lipid is a *phospholipid*. Phospholipids differ from the triglycerides because they contain two fatty acids and one phosphorous component. An example of a phospholipid is lecithin, an emulsifier. Emulsifiers dissolve in both fat and water and thereby help keep oil and water in products like salad dressing from separating. Some of the ingredients in processed baked products are emulsifiers.

The third type of lipid is a *sterol*. The most familiar one is chole*sterol*. Cholesterol, like all lipids, is a component of the body's cells. Its main function in the body is to help bile absorb fat from the intestine. Plants do not use fat, so they do not need cholesterol. Cholesterol is, therefore, found only in animal foods.

FATS IN DIGESTION

Lipids are the most concentrated energy source, yielding 9 Calories per gram. From Figure 3.1, we see that they function as part of the body structure. We can easily see stored fat, called *adipose* tissue, on our bodies. Adipose tissue, like insulation, helps maintain body core temperature. It also protects vital organs from blows to the body.

Through the processes of digestion and absorption, lipids are transported through the bloodstream. Not all lipids in the bloodstream come from the foods we eat. The liver can make both triglycerides and cholesterol. This raises the health question of whether fat and cholesterol in the food we eat can cause or contribute to chronic diseases. The liver produces cholesterol from particles of saturated fatty acids; this explains the current concern about eating foods containing saturated fats. Foods that are labeled "cholesterol-free" may only be free of animal fats. They can still contain the highly saturated vegetable oils—palm or coconut—that may contribute to higher blood-cholesterol levels. Other foods such as peanut butter may be very high in total fat but be low in saturated fat and contain no cholesterol. Look for the amount of total fat and saturated fat in a product, not just the cholesterol.

Which is a more important concern: cholesterol or saturated fat?

FATS IN BAKING

The critical factor for baked products and health concerns is the proportion of polyunsaturated, monounsaturated, and saturated fats in baked products. Have you considered substituting one type of fat for another? Saturated fats have a high smoke point (the point at which a fat or oil begins to smoke). This is one reason they have been used for years to fry foods such as french fries, donuts and popcorn. Flavor is another reason saturated fats are used—butter and beef tallow, for example, are saturated fats. A more unsaturated oil such as canola or soybean has a lower smoke point, meaning that it will burn at a lower temperature. Products containing these oils also have a different flavor. If a less saturated oil is used for high-temperature frying but not changed regularly, it will begin to break down; it will accept more hydrogen and become more saturated.

Saturated fats like lard shorten the gluten (protein) strands of flour, creating a finer, creamier texture. Substituting with mono- or polyunsaturated fats affects the traditional texture of baked products, a problem discussed in Chapter 6.

THE NON-ENERGY NUTRIENTS

VITAMINS

Today any large convenience store, grocery store, or drug store presents its customers with a vast array of bottled vitamins. Millions of dollars are spent annually on claims that promise more energy, less stress, quickness of mind and body—in summary, better health. In reality, vitamins provide no energy by themselves. They do facilitate the release of energy from the energy nutrients. All natural vitamins are organic substances, meaning that they are found in living things—plants or animals. Vitamins can also be synthesized in the chemistry laboratory. Whether they come from organic or synthetic sources, vitamins are used by the body equally efficiently.

TYPES OF VITAMINS AND THEIR SOURCES

There are two categories of vitamins: fat-soluble and water soluble. *Fat-soluble* means, of course, that the vitamin is soluble in fat and is therefore carried with lipids. The four fat-soluble vitamins—A, D, E, and K—are stored in the body, so daily intakes of the vitamin may vary without causing a deficiency. Excessive amounts of any of these four can be toxic. Fat-soluble vitamins are often found in food sources that have a higher fat content or are brightly colored. (see Table 3.1). Most vitamins are listed on nutrition labels in milligrams (mg). However, the fat-soluble vitamin A can be listed both as International Units (IU) or retinol equivalents (RE). In keeping with current philosophy, the vitamin A content is listed as retinol equivalents (REs) in the nutritional breakdown of the recipes in this book. It is simply a way of expressing the amount of vitamin A activity in the food.

Water-soluble vitamins include the B complexes and vitamin C. The human body stores only minimal amounts of water-soluble vitamins. Deficiency symptoms occur more quickly because these vitamins are not stored.

TABLE 3.1
Bakery Food Sources of Fat-Soluble Vitamins

Vitamin	Food Source
A	Bright yellow or orange: carrots, winter squash, pumpkin, apricot, egg yolk, sweet potato Fortified dairy products: milk, butter, margarines, cheddar cheese.
D	Animal products: all fortified milk, egg yolk
E	Nuts: sunflower seeds, almonds, peanuts, sweet potatoes, cooking oils
K	Some meats and green leafy vegetables

For food sources of water soluble vitamins, see Table 3.2. Approximately 40 percent of the population takes vitamin and mineral supplements, despite the fact that there is little evidence to support this practice if one is healthy and eats a balanced diet. Considering the consequences of toxic doses, the baking industry should promote dietary improvements through the increased use of healthful ingredients in baked products.

VITAMINS IN BAKING

Food preparation and storage techniques affect the vitamin content of food. It is well-known that excess cooking water and high temperatures cause vitamin loss. In baking, vitamin loss can be diminished by keeping dairy

TABLE 3.2
Bakery Food Sources of Water-Soluble Vitamins

Vitamin	Food Source
C	Fruits and vegetables: citrus fruits and juices, strawberries, raspberries, potatoes, fresh tomatoes
B_1 (Thiamin)	Sunflower seeds, bran cereal
B_2 (Riboflavin)	Milk and milk products, eggs, enriched or whole grain bread
B_3 (Niacin)	Milk and milk products, most grains
B_6 (Pyridoxine)	Legumes (dried beans or peas), bananas, potatoes, carrots
Folacin	Sweet potatoes, oranges and orange juice, oatmeal, wheat germ
B_{12} (Cyanocobalamin)	Eggs, milk products, yogurt, cottage cheese, American and Cheddar cheeses
Biotin	Nuts: peanuts, walnuts, pecans, peanut butter; Dairy: eggs, milk; Fruit: strawberries, bananas, peaches, raisins; Vegetables: tomatoes, potatoes
Pantothenic Acid	Eggs, milk and milk products, dried beans, sweet potatoes, bananas

TABLE 3.3
Nutrients Lost During Processing of White
Flour

Vitamins	Minerals
Thiamin*	Iron*
Riboflavin*	Magnesium
Niacin*	Copper
Vitamin B_6	Calcium
Folic acid	Zinc
Pantothenic acid	Manganese
Vitamin E	Potassium
Dietary Fiber	

* Nutrients replaced with enrichment

products such as milk at a constant, cold temperature. Direct light destroys riboflavin, a B vitamin in milk. Thawing and refreezing cause nutrient, quality, and flavor loss.

Grains are an excellent source of vitamins, but processing results in vitamin and mineral losses. Whole-grain cereals complete with the germ and outer bran are better sources of B vitamins and vitamin E than their processed counterparts are. To help replace vitamins and minerals lost during milling, products may be enriched or fortified. *Enrichment* is the process of replacing thiamin, riboflavin, niacin, and iron lost during the milling process. However, enrichment does not completely replace lost vitamins and minerals, as shown in Table 3.3. Preparing whole-grain products is one way to offer added nutrition.

Switching from refined grains does have some negative effects. Storage life of the whole grain is decreased because of the lipid-rich germ. Whole grains also affect the texture and cooking properties of baked products.

Fortification is the process of adding any nutrient to food, even if it did not originally contain the nutrient. Fortification long protected people from specific deficiency diseases such as anemia or rickets. Today, fortified products range from candy bars and cereal to orange juice. However, the emphasis seems to be on marketing to take advantage of the current health interest, rather than on preventing deficiency diseases.

MINERALS

When food is metabolized, the carbohydrates, fats, proteins, and vitamins fade into the air, water is formed, and ashes are left behind. These ashes are the minerals. Since the body is a combination of carbohydrates, fats, proteins, vitamins, water, and minerals, we, too, leave behind this mineral residue. More than one-third of our daily required nutrients are minerals needed for building the body and keeping it healthy. In a healthy 150-pound individual, five pounds can be attributed just to minerals. Most people are probably familiar with the mineral iron and its role in the formation of hemoglobin in the red blood cells. Sodium and chlorine (as chloride ions—hence the name *sodium chloride*) make up common table salt. Calcium, an important component of bones and teeth, is also required for bone strength. The past three decades of research produced much information about the teamwork of minerals; they interact with one another, so imbalances may have serious side effects. When an excess of one mineral is taken, the absorption of another may be affected. Zinc supplements decrease the absorption of iron and copper. Excess calcium affects the absorption of iron, zinc, and magnesium. Table 3.4 shows the minerals for which a recommended dietary allowance (RDA) has been established, as well as nine other minerals with an estimated safe and adequate daily range known as a *provisional RDA*. As research continues in the area of essential minerals, others will probably be added to this list. The minerals discussed in this section were selected because of their contribution to bakery products and current health concerns.

THE ROLE OF MINERALS IN THE BODY

Sodium and potassium are important in maintaining the body's fluid volume and balance. They work together—sodium outside the cell and potassium inside the cell—to maintain water pressure. When they are imbalanced, fluid retention and thus higher blood pressure can result. Because salt is 40 percent sodium by weight, it is easy to understand why decreasing salt is recommended for those with high blood pressure.

TABLE 3.4
Minerals for Which Consumption Guidelines Have Been Established

RDAs	Estimated RDAs*	Minimum Requirements**
Calcium	Copper	Potassium
Phosphorus	Manganese	Chlorine
Magnesium	Fluoride	Sodium
Iron	Chromium	
Iodine	Molybdenum	
Zinc		
Selenium		

* Estimated safe and adequate daily dietary intakes (population average).
** Estimated minimum requirement of healthy persons.

Calcium is one of the major minerals in bones, and dietary calcium is utilized by the body for bone formation. As the body ages, bone formation slows and, for some, bone density decreases, resulting in a condition known as *osteoporosis*. Calcium also plays a role in muscle function, blood clotting, and possibly in preventing high blood pressure.

Lack of one important dietary mineral, iron, continues to be the number one nutrient deficiency in the United States. A serious iron deficiency results in anemia. Anemia is characterized by small, pale red blood cells. Hemoglobin is a protein molecule in red blood cells that contains iron. When iron is not present in adequate amounts, less oxygen is carried by the hemoglobin to the body tissues. One then feels tired and has subnormal energy levels.

MINERALS IN BAKING

Enrichment and fortification have played an important role in providing essential dietary minerals. Most grain products are the primary dietary iron source, because most flour and cereals are iron-enriched. In the last 10 years, food manufacturers have added calcium to an assortment of food products, including cereals and flour. Even without the added calcium, bakery products contribute approximately 12 percent of the calcium in the American diet. Since we are urged to increase our dietary iron and calcium intakes, we can certainly look to bakery products as an important source of these minerals.

However, decreasing sodium is also a health recommendation. Grain products account for the single highest contributor of dietary sodium in the United States. Even though sodium plays an important role in yeast bread production, much of the sodium in grain products comes from chemicals added during processing—for example, salt, dough conditioners, sodium bicarbonate (baking soda), and baking powder all contribute sodium. Bakery products *can* be prepared with less salt and therefore less sodium. Appendix A includes such recipes.

WATER

When people are asked to name the essential nutrients, most of them forget water. Yet it comprises the largest part of our bodies and is the largest component of our diets. As one might guess, water helps to cool the body and is the basis of the transportation system for nutrients. It also aids in the release of energy from food and is needed for chemical reactions to occur within the body. The average 140-pound person contains about 12 gallons of water. It is nearly impossible to meet our dietary requirement for water from food. Bakery products provide only a very small percentage of water.

PRACTICAL ASPECTS OF NUTRIENTS IN BAKING

Nutrients are components of food, and understanding the Calorie content can help one understand food products. Butter and oils are fats and therefore provide 9 Calories per gram. Flour is mostly carbohydrate and provides 4 Calories per gram. In a recipe calling for a pound of flour and a pound of butter, you could roughly figure the calorie Content:

$$1 \text{ pound } = 454 \text{ grams}$$

$$454 \text{ grams } \times 9 \text{ Calories per gram } = 4,086 \text{ Calories from fat}$$

$$454 \text{ grams } \times 4 \text{ Calories per gram } = 1,816 \text{ Calories from carbohydrate}$$

In Figure 3.6, common baking ingredients are organized according to the nutrients they provide.

FIGURE 3.6
Examples of nutrients in baking ingredients

Carbohydrates (4 Cal/g)	Proteins (4 Cal/g)	Fats and oils (9 Cal/g)
Starches	Gelatin	Butter
Flour	Eggs*	Lard
Cornstarch	Milk*	Vegetable oils
Waxy maize	Cream*	Shortenings
Instant starches	Cheese*	Margarines
Sweeteners		Chocolate
Granulated sugar		
Brown sugar	**Vitamins or minerals**	
Confectioner's sugar	Enriched flour	
Corn syrup	Whole wheat flour	
Honey	Dairy products	
Invert sugar	Fruits and juices	
Fructose	Nuts and seeds	
Glucose	Salt	
Molasses	Eggs	
Malt syrup	Molasses	
	Pumpkin	

* Also contains fat.

How do these nutrients affect your loaf of bread? Let's examine the nutritional contributions of the ingredients in a simple bread recipe:

Ingredient	Nutritional Contribution
Yeast	Provides B vitamins and is the leavening.
Milk	Contributes B vitamins, minerals, protein, Calories, and water, which contributes moisture.
Sugar	A simple carbohydrate that contributes sweetness and Calories and aids in the browning reaction.
Butter	A fat that contributes Calories and taste and helps to make a softer crumb.
Salt	A mineral compound that adds flavor and inhibits the development of gluten.
Flour	A complex carbohydrate that provides structure, Calories, and fiber.
Eggs	Contribute fat, protein, and Calories; when protein is heated, it coagulates and provides support for the structure of the baked bread.

As you work with the recipes in this text, you can begin to appreciate the dual purpose of nutrients—to provide the necessary structure and appearance of your product, and, subsequently, the structure and appearance of you.

BIBLIOGRAPHY

"Americans to Make Lighter Choices in the '90s" *Calorie Control Commentary.* Spring 1990, Vol. 12, No. 1.

Brown, Judith E. *The Science of Human Nutrition.* New York: Harcourt Brace Jovanovich, 1990.

Hodges, Carol A. *Culinary Nutrition for Foodservice Professionals.* New York: Van Nostrand Reinhold, 1989.

McDonald, J.T. "Vitamin and Mineral Supplement Use in the United States." *Clinical Nutrition* Vol. 5, pp. 27–33. 1986.

National Research Council. *Recommended Dietary Allowances, 10th Edition.* National Academy Press, Washington, D.C., 1989.

Nieman, David, Diane E. Butterworth, Catherine Nieman. *Nutrition.* Dubuque, IA: Wm. C. Brown, 1990.

"Position of the American Dietetic Association: Vegetarian diets," *Journal of The American Dietetic Association,* Vol. 88, No. 3, pp. 351–355, 1988.

Subcommittee on the Tenth Edition of the RCAs Food and Nutrition Board, Commission on Life Sciences, National Research Council, *Recommonded Dietary Allowances*, Washington DC: National Academy Press, 1989, 81–87.

The Surgeon General's Report on Nutrition and Health. USDHHS (PHS) Publication No. 88-50211, Washington, DC, 1988.

ACTIVITIES

1. In a recipe for peanut butter cookies there are 25 grams of carbohydrate, 5 grams of protein and 10 grams of fat. Review the Calories per gram provided by these three nutrients and calculate the total Calories for the recipe. If the recipe makes 3 dozen cookies, how many Calories are there in each cookie?_____

Protein	5 grams	_____	Calories
Carbohydrate	25 grams	_____	Calories
Protein	10 grams	_____	Calories
		_____	Total Calories

2. Identify each different type and form of sugar you use in the bakery.

Example *white sugar*_____   *disaccharide*_____

_____   _____

_____   _____

_____   _____

4 NUTRITIONAL GUIDELINES DIETARY RECOMMENDATIONS

We become what we eat when nutrients from food are metabolized by our bodies. In Chapter 2, reasons for food choices were discussed. As we have become an industrialized nation, however, we have lost control over what we eat. No longer does our daily food supply come from our garden. We choose from over 15,000 foods in the local supermarket, and we eat away from home each week. How do we know how many nutrients we need, and how can we translate that information into wise choices at the supermarket, the bakery, or the restaurant? The U.S. Department of Health and Human Services published a report in 1990 entitled *Healthy People 2000.* This report describes a strategy for improving the nation's health by the year 2000. One of 21 priorities identified in *Healthy People 2000* is improved nutrition. Achievement of these goals requires individual and industry action. This chapter addresses four standards established to help us interpret information and evaluate the quality of our diets: the *Recommended Dietary Allowances,* the *Daily Food Guides,* and the *Dietary Guidelines* or *The Healthy American Diet.*

RECOMMENDED DIETARY ALLOWANCES

In 1943, the National Research Council of the National Academy of Sciences established the *Recommended Dietary Allowances* (RDA). These standards were established to provide Americans with guidelines for attaining good nutrition. They are updated approximately every five years to incorporate new research regarding nutritional needs. The Research Council also established qualifications for the use of the RDA:

1. The RDA is for population groups over a period of time, not for individuals on a daily basis.
2. The RDA is for healthy populations.

3.   The RDA is to be met through a variety of foods, not through fortification of products or supplementation.

The RDAs are used as the basis of the *Daily Food Guides,* which are well-established guides for food selection. Schools, hospitals, health care facilities, and the military use the RDA for planning menus and purchasing food supplies. The standard fortification policy for white bread is based on the RDA. The use of the RDA on food labels is explained in Chapter 5. However, the RDA does not address the current concern of the relationship between diet and disease.

DAILY FOOD GUIDES

The *Daily Food Guides* have been published by the United States Department of Agriculture (USDA) since the early 1900s, with revisions in 1943, 1958, and 1979. The original purpose of the guide was to help the homemaker plan meals to obtain balance and variety, and to ensure adequate protein, carbohydrate, and fat intake in the diet. The *Daily Food Guide* today has four food

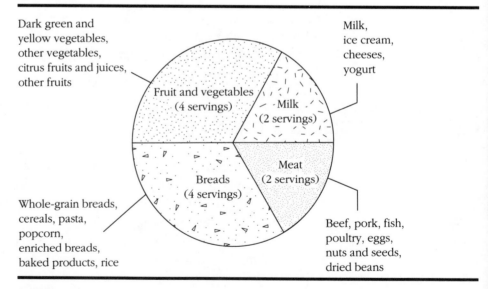

FIGURE 4.1
Daily food guide with four food groups

groups from which to select a recommended number of servings, as demonstrated in Figure 4.1. A fifth group—fats, sweets, and alcohol—is not included because there is no recommendation for servings from this group.

The *Daily Food Guide* directs one to choose a variety of foods (something from each group) but fails to help one select a healthful diet. In grade school most people probably learned the food groups, but people have failed to learn proper serving sizes or the foods comprising each group. Two servings of meat (approximately six ounces total) per day are recommended. One double burger from the local fast-food restaurant meets this requirement, yet it's viewed as only one serving. Adding another serving of meat to this increases one's intake of saturated fat. In 1984 Dr. Helen Guthrie published a study showing that only one-third of her research group consumed a diet adequate in vitamin E, vitamin B_6, iron, and zinc. These young adults were following the *Daily Food Guide*.

THE DIETARY GUIDELINES

During the late 1960s and early 1970s, research was beginning to relate more diseases to dietary trends. The U.S. Senate Select Committee on Nutrition and Human Needs published *Dietary Goals* focusing on balancing nutritional excesses rather than on nutritional needs. This set of seven dietary goals provoked much controversy among nutrition professionals, food activist groups, and health organizations. They were retitled *The Dietary Guidelines* in 1980 and revised in 1985. In 1988 the Surgeon General issued a report showing evidence that nutritional excesses were responsible for much of the illness and death in the United States. In 1989, in an effort to reach a consensus in support of the Surgeon General's report, nine health organizations and professional groups agreed on their own dietary guidelines. Entitled *The Healthy American Diet,* the guidelines address dietary concerns related to prevention and control of cancer, diabetes, heart and blood vessel disease, and stroke. The six guidelines are intended to encourage all Americans over the age of two to improve their health through diet and weight control. They are similar to the 1990 edition of the *Dietary Guidelines for Americans,* which recommends the same basic concepts as the 1985 edition. Table 4.1 shows the changes in *The Dietary Guidelines* from 1985 to 1990. Included for comparison is *The Healthy American Diet.*

The *Healthy American Diet* includes three additional guidelines directed toward specific population groups and identifies individual nutrients. Sugar consumption was addressed in *The Dietary Guidelines; The Healthy American*

TABLE 4.1
Summary of Changes in Dietary Recommendations

Dietary Guidelines for Americans, 1985	The Healthy American Diet, 1989*	Dietary Guidelines for Americans, 1990
Eat a variety of foods.	Eat a nutritionally adequate diet consisting of a variety of foods.	Eat a variety of foods.
Maintain desirable weight.	Achieve and maintain a reasonable body weight.	Maintain healthy weight.
Avoid too much fat, saturated fat, and cholesterol.	Reduce fat consumption, especially saturated fat and cholesterol.	Choose a diet low in fat, saturated fat, and cholesterol.
Eat foods with adequate starch and fiber.	Increase consumption of complex carbohydrates and fiber.	Choose a diet with plenty of vegetables, fruits, and grain products.
Avoid too much sugar.	To avoid dental cavities, ensure access to fluoride and moderate between-meal use of foods containing sugar.	Use sugars in moderation.
Avoid too much sodium.	Reduce intake of sodium.	Use salt and sodium in moderation.
If you drink alcoholic beverages do so in moderation.	Consume alcohol in moderation, if at all.	If you drink alcoholic beverages do so in moderation.
	To help prevent osteoporosis, increase consumption of foods high in calcium, particularly lowfat dairy products.	
	To help prevent iron deficiency anemia, consume good sources of iron such as lean red meat, fish, and iron-enriched cereals.	

* Developed by the American Heart Association; the American Dietetic Association; the American Academy of Pediatrics; the American Cancer Society; the American Diabetes Association; the Centers for Disease Control; the National Heart, Lung, and Blood Institute; and the U.S. Departments of Agriculture and Health and Human Services.

Diet included recommendations for two additional minerals: increased intake of calcium-rich foods to help prevent osteoporosis and increased intake of iron-rich foods to help prevent iron deficiency anemia. One should examine these guidelines individually to understand the changes in the American diet and the rationale behind *The Healthy American Diet*.

1. *Eat a nutritionally adequate diet consisting of a variety of foods.* In Chapter 3, we see that nutrients from dietary sources must come from a variety

of foods. Eating a variety of foods increases the possibility of obtaining all the necessary nutrients. Because each food supplies several nutrients, substituting vitamin and mineral supplements for a healthy diet may cause a nutritional imbalance.

2. *Achieve and maintain a reasonable body weight.* Obesity is one of the most serious nutritional problems in the United States. Of the ten leading causes of death in the United States, five list obesity as a risk factor. Although the term *obesity* is easily defined, the cause and cure are not easily identified. Health professionals support the theory that some obese people consume excess Calories. From Chapter 3 we know that Calories come from the protein, carbohydrate, and fat content of foods. We also know that there has been an increase in the amount of fat in the American diet; today, approximately 40 percent of all Calories come from fat in foods. In an effort to determine what food selections contribute to this trend, the *National Health and Nutrition Examination Survey* reports the major contributors of Calories in the American diet. Baked products such as white bread, rolls, crackers, doughnuts, and cookies are a major source of Calories. If we are to manage our weight while continuing to consume baked products, the baked products will have to be lower in fat.

3. *Reduce fat consumption, especially saturated fat and cholesterol.* We know from the discussion of lipids in Chapter 1 that fats and oils contribute the highest number of Calories per gram. When looking at food consumption trends, we find that fat consumption is higher now than at any previous time this century. As mentioned above, the average American's diet derives approximately 40 percent of its Calories from fat: 15 to 20 percent saturated, 15 to 20 percent monounsaturated, and 5 to 7 percent polyunsaturated. This pattern of fat consumption has been related to heart disease, some cancers, diabetes, and obesity.

Where does our dietary fat come from? Figure 4.2 shows sources of dietary fat and the change in fat consumption since 1910. One should note that plant oils, margarine, and shortening, rather than animal fats, have increased total fat consumption. Chapter 3 mentions that coconut and palm oils are saturated and some margarines and shortening are monounsaturated. The American Heart Association recommends that one's daily caloric intake from fat be less than 30 percent—less than 10 percent saturated, 10 percent monounsaturated, and 10 percent polyunsaturated. As Figure 4.2 demonstrates, we have as a society already decreased our intake of saturated fats from butter and lard; these fats, however, have been replaced by the highly saturated coconut and palm oils. Consumers want to know the fat content of bakery products they purchase. Table 4.2 shows the

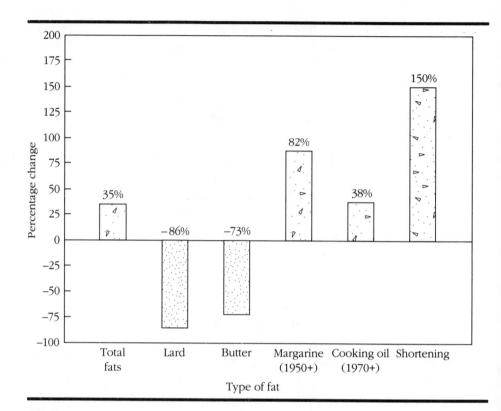

FIGURE 4.2

Changes in total consumption of fat from 1910 to 1985

percentage of Calories from fat of various foods used in or produced in the bakery.

With the increase in consumption of other polyunsaturated oils such as those from corn and soybeans, it becomes clear that we need to replace coconut and palm oils with food sources of monounsaturated fats, including olive oil and canola oil. Cholesterol, of course, has been related to heart disease. The American Heart Association recommends consumption of less than 300 mg of cholesterol per day, yet our current consumption is twice that amount. Much of this—36 percent of the total amount—comes from eggs. In summary, what do these fat and cholesterol recommendations mean to the baking industry?

1. Use less total fat in bakery products.
2. Use fewer whole eggs, as cholesterol is found mostly in the egg yolk.
3. Replace traditional fat sources with more monounsaturated and polyun-saturated fats such as unsaturated plant oils.

TABLE 4.2
Percentage of Calories from Fat in Selected Bakery Foods

Percentage	Food
90–100	Margarine, butter, vegetable oils, mayonnaise
80–90	Walnuts, cream cheese, sour cream
70–80	Cheddar cheese, peanut butter, sunflower seeds
60–70	Eggs, swiss cheese
50–60	Danish pastry, chocolate chip cookie
40–50	Whole milk, doughnut, croissant, cream pie, ice cream
30–40	2% milk, apple pie, cottage cheese
20–30	Crackers
10–20	Most breads, 1% milk, low-fat cottage cheese
Less than 10	Plain potato, cornflakes, bagel, egg white, fruits, most vegetables, skim milk

4. *Increase consumption of complex carbohydrates and fiber.* Currently, as a population we are eating an imbalance of carbohydrates. We have not only decreased our total carbohydrate consumption throughout this century, but we have switched to more sugar and less starch and fiber (see Figure 4.3). This increase in sugar leads to an increase in foods providing Calories but few minerals and vitamins. These "empty Calorie" foods take the place of other more nutritious foods and may increase the incidence of obesity. Dietary recommendations for the prevention of cancer and heart disease also include eating more fruits, vegetables, and whole grains, which provide complex carbohydrates and fiber. The *1990 Dietary Guidelines* propose eating three servings of vegetables and three servings of fruit each day.

Since 1970 we have increased our consumption of fresh fruits and vegetables and grain products such as pasta and cereals. Even with this increase, we are not getting the recommended 50 percent or more of our Calories from complex carbohydrates and 20 to 30 grams of dietary fiber per day. One way to help meet this goal is to eat six or more servings of whole grain products each day. The baking industry can meet this challenge by taking these easy steps:

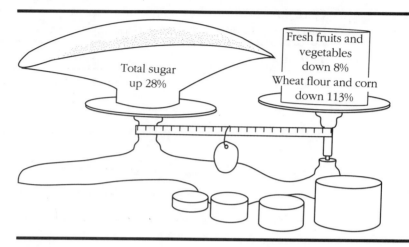

FIGURE 4.3
Imbalance in U.S. carbohydrate consumption between 1910 and 1985

1. Use more whole grains in baked products.
2. Use fewer simple sugars and sweeteners.

5. *Reduce intake of sodium.* In a recent poll conducted by the Roper Organization, 70 percent of those responding said they were concerned about the amount of salt in their diets. As mentioned in Chapter 3, salt is 40 percent sodium by weight, and sodium plays a role in maintaining normal water balance; high dietary intakes of sodium are thus associated with hypertension and otherwise high blood pressure. As Americans continue to be concerned about sodium, they are finding that much of it comes from processed food. Bakery products represent nearly 25 percent of all sodium consumed; one-half of that comes from white bread, rolls, and crackers. Recipes in this book provide the reader with the opportunity to offer customers a lower-sodium alternative.

6. *Dental cavities—moderate between-meal use of foods containing sugar.* The relationship between sugar intake and tooth decay has been proven beyond question. There is a direct relationship between the number of grams of sugar consumed per day and the average number of decayed, missing or filled teeth. This recommendation suggests limiting sugary snacks. Sugary foods could be eaten in moderation with a meal because sugar is more likely to be cleaned off the teeth when eaten with other foods. Most people do not clean their teeth after sugary between-meal snacks, so the sugar stays in their mouths longer. This causes more acid to be produced by the mouth

bacteria and promotes tooth decay. An added benefit to eating fewer sugary foods is a reduction in caloric intake, as many foods high in sugar also provide fat.

The single greatest contributor of sugar to our diet is soft drinks. However, soft drinks contribute only about 3.5 percent of our total calories, while doughnuts and cookies contribute 6 percent. Part of this difference is the fat content of the latter. The other part is the increased use of high-fructose corn syrup, resulting in higher intakes of sugar. Figure 4.4 shows the increase in intake of total sweeteners since 1970 and the breakdown of refined sugars, corn sweeteners, and non-caloric sweeteners according to use. This book provides recipes for reduced-sugar or sugar-free bakery products. The American Diabetic Association recommends that products with 1 to 3 teaspoons of sugar, or 5 to 15 grams, per serving be selected "occasionally" or limited to one per day. Products containing over 3 teaspoons-per serving are considered high in sugar. Products with less than one teaspoon of sugar, or less than 5 grams, need not have any special notation. The chart in Appendix A helps identify which recipes meet this recommendation.

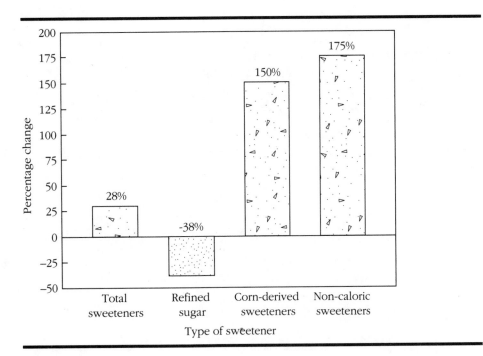

FIGURE 4.4

Types of sweeteners and changes in total consumption since 1910

7. *Osteoporosis—increase consumption of foods high in calcium, particularly lowfat dairy products.* Calcium is a mineral that contributes to the hardness of bones. Osteoporosis is an age-related disease resulting in decreased bone strength due to increased porosity. Women are more at risk than men, but loss in bone mass occurs for all people as they age. The consumption of calcium in the United States is below the recommended level of 800 mg per day. Figure 4.5 shows the contribution of bakery products to the calcium intake of the U.S. diet. With whole wheat and white breads, rolls and crackers contributing 10 percent of our daily calcium intake, we should promote eating more bread!

8. *Iron-deficiency anemia—consume good sources of iron such as lean red meat, fish and iron-enriched cereals.* There are four populations at risk for iron deficiency in the United States:

1. Infants, birth to six months
2. Boys and girls during early adolescence
3. Women, puberty through menopause
4. Women during pregnancy

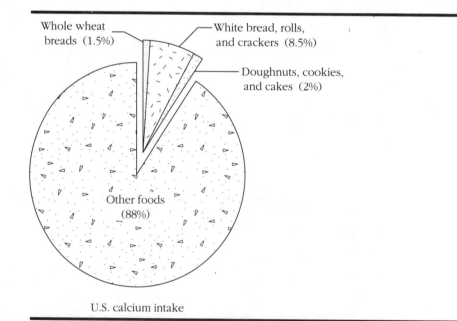

U.S. calcium intake

FIGURE 4.5
Contribution of bakery products to U.S. calcium intake

Iron intake for these four groups is inadequate. Even though this recommendation does not mention bakery products specifically, we cannot overlook the contribution of bakery products to iron in the U.S. diet (see Figure 4.6). White bread, rolls, and crackers contribute more iron to the U.S. diet than any other food source because they are made with iron-enriched flour, as described in Chapter 3. With enrichment, iron deficiency has declined in the past 15 years, yet it is still the most common nutritional deficiency in the world.

In conclusion, *The Healthy American Diet* is a set of guidelines developed because Americans still need to improve their diets. How can we use these guidelines to elevate bakery products to a more significant role and meet the year 2000 health objectives?

1. Provide healthier alternatives with less fat and less sugar.
2. Promote the nutrient contribution of calcium and iron in bread products.
3. Inform customers of the recommendation to include six servings of grain products a day.

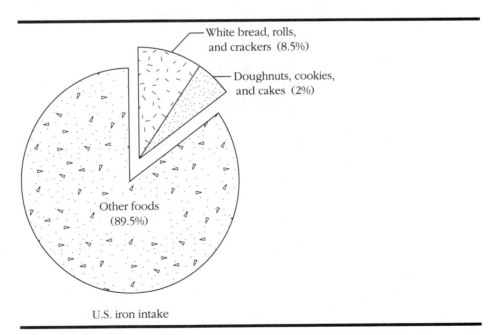

FIGURE 4.6

Contribution of bakery products to U.S. iron intake

BIBLIOGRAPHY

Block, G., C. M. Dresser, A. M. Hartman, and M. D. Carroll. "Nutrient Sources in the American Diet: Quantitative Data from the NHANES II Survey." *American Journal of Epidemiology,* Vol. 122, pp. 27–40, 1985.

Britt, Elena C., "Healthy People 2000," *Journal of Nutrition Education,* Vol. 22, No. 5, 239–240, 19XX.

"Dietary Guidelines for Healthy American Adults: A Statement for Physicians and Health Professionals." Nutrition Committee, American Heart Association. Dallas: American Heart Association, 1986.

Guthrie, H. A. "Selection and Quantification of Typical Food Proportions by Young Adults." *Journal of the American Dietetic Association,* Vol. 84, pp. 1440–44, 1984.

Nieman, David, Diane Butterworth, and Catherine Nieman. *Nutrition.* Dubuque, IA: Wm. C. Brown Publishers. 1990.

"Nine Major Organizations Agree on *The Healthy American Diet.*" *ADA Courier,* Vol. 29, No. 8, p. 2, 1990.

"Relaxing the rules." *Diabetes Forecast.* pp. 9–10, June 1989.

Report of Advisory Committee on the Dietary Guidelines for Americans. *Nutrition Today.* Vol. 25, No. 4, pp. 44–45, 1990.

U.S. Department of Agriculture, Human Nutrition Information Service. *Nationwide Food Consumption Survey. Continuing Survey of Food Intakes by Individuals: Women 19–50 Years and Their Children 1–5 Years, 1 Day,* U.S. Department of Agriculture, Rept. No. 85-1; *Men 19–50 Years, 1 Day,* U.S. Department of Agriculture, Rept. No. 85-3.

ACTIVITIES

1. Select ten of the most popular recipes you currently use in the bakery.
2. Record the source of fat or oil used in each product; include the type of oil used for frying deep-fried products.
3. Identify each type of fat as saturated (S), monounsaturated (M), or polyunsaturated (P) for the ten products. Check the list in Chapter 3 if you're not sure.
4. Count the number of S's, M's and P's. This number times 10 will be your percentage of products with a particular type of fat. For instance, if you have 7 saturated, that will be 70 percent with saturated fat on your list. Compare these percentages to the American Heart Association recommendations.
5. Do you need to make any ingredient changes? What changes can you suggest? _____

Product	Source of Fat	Type of Fat
Example: *Danish*	*butter*	*S*
1.		
2.		
3.		
4.		
5.		
6.		
7.		
8.		
9.		
10.		

5

LABELS

A GUIDE THROUGH
THE LABEL MAZE

Bakery products can have a nutritional advantage because of the compatibility of their ingredients with *The Dietary Guidelines,* as discussed in Chapter 4. Bakers can use this information in promoting bakery products just as other industries do: Put it on the label! The National Food Processor's Association (NFPA) conducted a food labeling survey of 1400 consumers in 1989. The results of this survey were as follows.

1. Consumers "always" or "sometimes" read the label before making a first-time purchase (79% of respondents).
2. Consumers say ingredient and nutrition information have a "great deal" or "some" influence in a purchase decision (83% of respondents).
3. Consumers mostly want information on sodium, fat, calories, cholesterol, and sugar.
4. Consumers want more information about relationships between food and health.
5. Consumers' primary reason for not reading labels is lack of understanding, not lack of interest.

This information corresponds to information from the American Dietetic Association (ADA) in its statement on food labels. ADA added complex carbohydrates, fiber, and calcium to the list of nutrients in item 3 of the list. The survey results support adding a nutrition label to influence 80 percent of one's customers. How can nutrition labeling be used to communicate with customers?

LABELS OF THE PAST

Since the early 1900s, the federal government has been involved in regulating food, including food labeling. In 1938, the Food and Drug Administration (FDA) enacted the Federal Food, Drug, and Cosmetic Act. This act specified the requirements for basic information on food labels (see Figure 5.1).

The FDA has authority over all packaged food products except for meat, poultry, and egg products. These fall under the jurisdiction of the U.S. Department of Agriculture.

Currently, some products do not contain a list of ingredients. These products qualify under a *standard of indentity* established by the FDA. This standard covers products that have a common name such as peanut butter, mayonnaise, or catsup. The FDA determines the ingredient listing—the recipe—for all products under the standard of identity. Anything added to the product that is not part of the standard ingredient listing must be listed on the label. The FDA adopted a standard of identity for over 300 foods. This exception for listing ingredients was eliminated in November 1990 by Congress (PL 101-535). As a result, consumers will get more complete information about the components of food they eat.

The FDA uses standards of identity to regulate the fortification of foods. The recent interest in fortifying foods with calcium is an example. When the Florida Citrus Commission asked the FDA to allow orange juice to be fortified with calcium, the FDA refused to sanction it; the fortification was

1. The name of the food	WHOLE WHEAT BREAD
2. Ingredient list	Ingredients: whole wheat, flour, water, corn sugar, wheat gluten, yeast, molasses, soybean oil, wheat germ, wheat bran, salt, honey, raisin syrup, calcium sulfate, potassium bromate.
3. Net contents or net weight	Net Weight: 24 oz. (1½ lb.) 680 grams
4. The name and place of business of the manufacturer, packer, or distributor	Better Baking Company General Office, Anywhere, USA, 11122

FIGURE 5.1
Basic information required on all food packages

not part of the standard for orange juice. Even so, calcium-fortified orange juice is available.

INGREDIENT LABELING

The labeling regulation requires manufactureres to list the ingredients on the lables of foods not covered by a standard. The ingredients must appear in descending order according to weight. For example, a cookie might show flour as the first ingredient because, by weight, it is the ingredient in greatest amount in the cookie.

An area of concern is a regulation known as *and/or* labeling. This regulation allows the label not to specifiy the exact composition of the product. However, *and/or* allows the manufacturer to use the least expensive product at the time of production. A common example of this is the use of *and/or* in listings with fats and oils in products in which they are not the predominant ingredient; the consumer has no indication of which one the product actually contains. Therefore, the consumer doesn't know whether the product contains a highly saturated fat such as coconut or palm oil or a less saturated fat such as cottonseed oil. An example is this ingredient listing from a cookie product:

> **Ingredients:** Enriched wheat flour, sugar, corn syrup, corn sweetener, cocoa, animal and vegetable shortening (lard and/or partially hydrogenated beef fat and/or palm oil and/or partially hydrogenated soybean oil), nonfat milk, gelatin, corn starch, sodium bicarbonate, chocolate, salt, potassium sorbate, lecithin, artificial flavor.

Because use of *and/or* is confusing and ambiguous, the FDA has proposed new rules in accordance with the 1990 law to clarify label language for consumers.

Currently, manufacturers must list food additives by name, except colors and flavorings, which need only be listed as artificial colors and natural or artificial flavor. Yellow dye no. 5 is an exception because of its association with allergies. As a result of the 1990 amendment, certified color additives are no longer exempt. Sulfites, another additive associated with allergies, must be listed on the label when used as a preservative. However, when used to condition dough in the making of cookies or bread, they do not have to be listed. Since the 1990 amendment, sulfite labeling will be required if a detectable amount is present in the finished product.

Nutrition Labeling

In 1969 the White House Conference on Food, Nutrition, and Health recommended that manufacturers add nutrition informatin to food labels. The FDA introduced nutrition labeling in 1971 to create public awareness of the nutrients in food. The policy required nutrition information only on products that were fortified or when the label made a nutrition claim. Nutrition labeling of other products was voluntary. Now, approximately 55 percent of food packages have some type of nutrition information in their labels.

On November 8, 1990, a law was passed to amend the Federal Food, Drug, and Cosmetic Act to prescribe nutrition labeling for foods. The FDA is currently writing rules to define procedures that food processing companies will have to follow. Fresh fruits and vegetables will have labels, as well as 20,000 other packaged food items. Bakeries will only be exempt from labeling the single service items sold over the counter; they will be entirely exempt if their annual sales are less than $500,000. Figure 5.2 lists the proposed required nutrition information, followed by a sample label.

To summarize, the new labels must include fat, cholesterol, total carbohydrates, complex carbohydrates, sugars, fiber, and saturated fat. The "Percentage of USRDA" column will become "Percent of Daily Value"

NUTRITION INFORMATION PER SERVING (REQUIRED)

1. Serving size (including measure, weight, and metric equivalents
2. Servings per container
3. Calories
4. Calories from fat
5. Grams of fat
6. Grams of saturated fat
7. Milligrams of cholesterol
8. Grams of total carbohydrates
9. Grams of complex carbohydrates
10. Grams of total sugar (including corn syrups, fruit syrups, honey, and sugar alcohols)
11. Grams of dietary fiber
12. Grams of protein
13. Milligrams of sodium
14. Percent of daily value (the median RDA for children age 4 to adult) for the following:
    Vitamin A
    Vitamin C
    Calcium
    Iron

(continued)

FIGURE 5.2
Basic nutrition label requirements per FDA interpretations, 1991

NUTRITION PROFILE (VOLUNTARY)

(Given in two values: (1) as percentage of daily value and (2) the actual total grams or milligrams of substance)

1. Fat
2. Saturated fatty acid
3. Unsaturated fatty acid
4. Cholesterol
5. Carbohydrate
6. Dietary fiber
7. Sodium
8. Potassium

SAMPLE LABEL FOR HERMITS (RECIPE ON P. 127)

Serving size: 1 oz (28 g)
Servings per container: 12
Calories (Energy): 93
Calories for Fat: 18
Fat: 2 g
Saturated Fatty Acid: <1 g
Cholesterol: 0 mg
Carbohydrate: 17 g
Complex carbohydrates: 10 g
Total sugar: 5 g
Dietary Fiber: 1 g
Protein: 2 g
Sodium: 98 mg

Percentage of Daily Value
Vitamin   A: 2%
Vitamin   C: 0
Calcium: 1%
Iron: 5%

Nutrition Profile

Component	Percentage of Daily Value	Daily Value
Fat	3	75 g
Saturated fatty acid	2	25 g
Unsaturated fatty acid	3	25 g
Cholesterol	0	300 g
Carbohydrates	5	325 g
Dietary fiber	3	25 g
Sodium	2	2400 mg
Potassium	2	3500 mg

FIGURE 5.2
(continued)

(see Appendix B). Reporting of thiamin, riboflavin, and niacin values will be voluntary. A new section relates cholesterol, carbohydrate, fiber, sodium, and potassium as a percentage of the amount recommended for a day. The proposed rules will correct misleading information regarding cholesterol. Today, a product can be advertised as "cholesterol-free" and still be high in saturated fat or total fat. The proposed rules allow the label to say "cholesterol-free" only on foods with less than 2 milligrams of cholesterol and less than 5 grams of fat and 2 grams of saturated fat per serving. The final rules go into effect in May 1993.

The standard serving sizes of bakery products would reflect the actual food consumed per occasion. The FDA established new serving sizes from information reported in the 1977 to 1987 Nationwide Food Consumption Survey (Table 5.1).

TABLE 5.1
Proposed Standard Serving Sizes for Bakery Products

Product	Standard Serving Size	Label Statement
Bread sticks	1 oz	1 oz (28 g)
Breads (excluding sweet quick type), biscuits, rolls, croissants, muffins, bagels	2 oz	2 oz (57 g)
Brownies	2 oz	2 oz (57 g)
Cake with icing, except cheesecake	3.5 oz	3.5 oz (98 g)
Cake without icing, except cheesecake	2 oz	2 oz (57 g)
Cheesecake	4 oz	4 oz (112 g)
Coffee cakes, doughnuts, Danish, sweet rolls, sweet quick breads	2.5 oz	2.5 oz (70 g)
Cookies, graham crackers, sandwich-type crackers	1 oz	1 oz (28 g)
Cracker, all other varieties	½ oz	½ oz (14 g)
French toast, pancakes	4 oz	4 oz (112 g)
Pies, cobblers, eclairs, turnovers, other pastries	4 oz	4 oz (112 g)
Waffles	3 oz	3 oz (84 g)

HEALTH CLAIMS AND LABEL LANGUAGE

As more people began using nutrition labeling, manufacturers took advantage of a new form of advertising: They used the product label to make a health claim. In 1987, the FDA proposed regulations for health claims on food that meet the following criteria:

- They must be truthful and not mislead the consumer
- They should show that good health results from a good diet over time, not a specific food
- Claims must be based on valid, reliable scientific evidence
- The product must also carry a nutrition label if it carries a nutrition claim

We can see how this changes a health claim about cholesterol. The original label stated, "Can Help Reduce Cholesterol." Under the new FDA guidelines, the label must read, "Can Help Reduce Cholesterol when part of a fat-modified, low-cholesterol diet." The American Dietetic Association believes that the use of health claims on food labels may help educate the public. However, it recommends strict monitoring of the language used for such purpose. It also suggests that the information be consistent with *The Dietary Guidelines*. The debate over the language and use of health claims on lables is not over. Bakeries can benefit from using product labels to make health claims. However, one should make sure that the claim conforms to the FDA regulations. See the Appendix for a guide to the recipes found in this text.

The FDA and the FTC (Federal Trade Commission) defined terms for calories, fat, cholesterol, salt, and sugar (see Table 5.2). However, the term *light* has not yet been defined. "Light" can mean less calories, less fat, less sodium, less sugar, or something completely different. In a recent grocery store survey, "lite" milk was placed next to 1 percent milk; however, according to the labels, there were no nutritional differences. With the new proposed labeling regulations that compare fat and sodium to a daily value, it may be easier to define the term *light*.

In the baking industry, we can use nutrition labels to help promote informed food choices. The recipes in Part II have nutrition information that could be used on a nutrition label. However, using the nutrition label as given means that one must follow the recipe exactly. To change one ingredient, one amount, or the serving size changes the formulation and

TABLE 5.2
Terms (Label Language) for Calories, Sugar, Salt, and Cholesterol

Term	Definition
Calorie	
Low calorie	Less than 40 calories per serving or 0.4 calories per gram of food
Reduced calorie	One-third fewer calories than the original product
Diet	Either the low-calorie or reduced-calorie requirement
Sugar	
Sugar-free	Does not contain sucrose but may contain other sweeteners (the 1990 labeling proposals would change this to include all sweeteners including sugar alcohols).
Naturally sweetened	This is not regulated, so product may contain fruit, fruit juices, or refined sweeteners
Salt	
Sodium-free	Contains less than 5 mg per serving
Very low sodium	Contains 35 mg or less per serving
Low sodium	Contains 140 mg or less per serving
Reduced sodium	Sodium is reduced by 75 percent of original
Unsalted or No salt added	No salt had been added during processing, but product may still contain sodium
Cholesterol	
Cholesterol-free	Contains less than 2 mg per serving
Low cholesterol	Less than 20 mg per serving
Reduced cholesterol	Contains 75% less cholesterol than the original product

therefore the nutrition information. Chapter 6 discusses how small changes in the ingredient formulation can make significant changes in the nutritional content.

BIBLIOGRAPHY

Federal Register. Department of Health and Human Services, July 19, 1990.

Federal Register. Department of Health and Human Services, June 21, 1991.

"Health claims on food labels: An American Dietetic Association perspective (ADA timely statement)." Legislative Highlights, *Journal of the American Dietetic Association* Vol. 88, No. 2, 1988.

Kessler, David A. "The Federal Regulation of Food Labeling." *New England Journal of Medicine,* Vol. 321, No. 11, pp. 752–756 1989.

"Labeling Update." *Walden Farms Newsletter,* Summer 1990.

"Light Labels Keep Shoppers in the Dark." *Environmental Nutrition,* Vol. 13, No. 8, p. 1 August 1990.

"Nutrition information on food labels (ADA timely statement)." ADA Reports *Journal of the American Dietetic Association* Vol. 89, p. 2, 1989.

Public Law 101-535, 101st Congress, November 8, 1990.

"What'll be on our food labels?" *Food Service Director,* September 1990.

ACTIVITIES

1. Select a recipe from this text and copy the ingredient label provided with the recipe.
2. Circle the required information on the label.
3. Underline the voluntary information provided.
4. Describe what would change on the product label if you changed the serving size of the product.

6 HEALTHFUL INGREDIENTS SUBSTITUTIONS AND MODIFICATIONS

What is a recipe but a list of ingredients? What are ingredients but the raw materials needed to make a product? The ingredients we choose affect every aspect of our bakery products, including taste, texture, and nutrition, as well as marketability and cost. We set a certain standard for our products and select ingredients to give us that predictable outcome. Why, today, do we choose certain ingredients over others? By what standards do we judge our bakery products? Over the last century bakers have created richer and sweeter bakery products, as evidenced by our increased consumption of fats and sugars. In the past, little value has been placed on nutrition. Is this a criterion that needs greater emphasis? When we accept nutrition as an important component of our bakery products, we can make informed choices in our ingredient selections that reflect the values of today's health-conscious consumers.

In the previous chapters, we reviewed the historical development of three important ingredients used in baking and the reasons behind our food choices. We have looked at principles of nutrition and how they can be applied to our baked products, and we examined an overview of dietary recommendations. In this chapter, we will translate *The Dietary Guidelines* into specific, healthful bakery ingredient choices. We will then compare the nutritional analyses of some formulas to show how substituting ingredients can have a positive effect on bakery products.

There are many ingredients we use to make our bakery products. Although they all have a specific purpose that provides a visible and concrete function, such as building structure, adding flavor, giving texture, or supplying color, the "invisible" function of providing nutritional value can no longer be ignored. Our bakery products can be healthy foods as well as delicious and attractive. How can this be accomplished? Let's take a look at common baking ingredients we now use, and then see what changes we can make to conform to the new guidelines.

BAKING INGREDIENTS

FLOURS

Most bakery products contain flour as the main ingredient because it provides needed structure and body. Wheat is the source for most flour. There are different types of wheat flours available. *Patent, clear, high gluten,* and *straight* flours are used in bread making because they are milled from a wheat berry that has more protein and therefore more strength. Bread flours offer the support needed for the expansion of gases during proofing and baking of yeast breads. Other types of wheat flour include pastry and cake flour. Each is milled from a wheat variety that has less protein and thus produces a softer flour. Cake flour is used mainly for fine-textured cakes, while pastry flour is generally used for cookies and pie crusts.

The milling process completely sifts out the bran and germ, leaving the starchy endosperm. Although using white flour may have some advantages, such as giving a whiter crumb and finer texture to products, using all parts of the wheat will give more nutritional value. Whole wheat flour not only contains more vitamins and trace minerals, but valuable fiber as well (see Figure 6.1). *The Dietary Guidelines* recommends increasing our consumption of fiber and eating whole grains is an excellent way to get more fiber. Whole-wheat or other whole-grain flours should be substituted for some or all of the white flour in recipes whenever possible. Whole-wheat pastry flour retains all the nutritional value of the whole grain, and, because it is milled from a soft wheat, it makes an excellent substitute for cake and pastry flour.

There are many other grains besides wheat that can be used in baking, although no other grain possesses the necessary gluten to make bread rise. However, other grain flours can replace part of the wheat flour to make tasty and nutritious yeast breads. In pastry making, gluten is not necessary—in fact, it is not desired—so other whole-grain flours can easily be substituted for part of the wheat flour. Cookies made with different flours (see Creative Cutout Cookies, p. 128) have unique flavors and are more nutritious than those made with only white flour. Although cakes are usually made with cake flour, those that require more body, such as carrot and applesauce, can successfully be made with whole-wheat pastry flour or other whole-grain flours. This substitution will produce a cake that is nutritionally superior to one made with white flour.

What other flours can be used in baking? Nutritionally similar to wheat, rye flour has been used traditionally in making rye breads, but it can also be used for cookies and some cakes. Buckwheat, with its distinct flavor, is

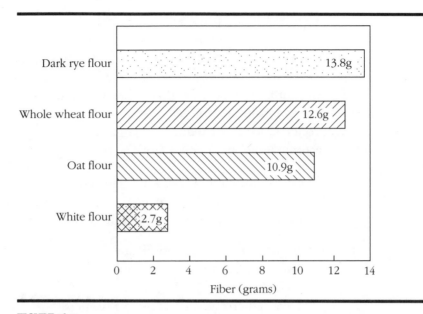

FIGURE 6.1
Dietary fiber content per 100 grams (3.5 oz) of different types of flour

another hearty grain that can be incorporated in breadmaking, along with barley, one of the first grains cultivated by humans. Oats are a versatile grain that impart a sweetness and moisture to breads, and are delicious in cookies, bars and even cakes. A new "old" grain recently rediscovered is amaranth, a native grain of the Americas, which has a high protein content. Another American grain—corn—can be used in bread making as well as in muffins and quick breads. Wheat, rye, oats, and barley are available as flours and also as flakes that can be easily added to cookie doughs. Don't limit yourself to just wheat flour. Try these and other whole grains in your formulas for additional nutritional value.

SUGARS

The sugar we use the most in baking is sucrose, or table sugar. It comes in a variety of forms—granulated, powdered, and brown. Available syrups include molasses, corn syrup, honey, and maple syrup. Sugar provides the following functions in baking:

1. Adds sweetness—its main purpose
2. Acts as a source of food for fermenting yeast in breads and rolls
3. Helps retain moisture, thus retarding the staling process
4. Imparts good color to crusts
5. Gives desired texture and grain

How much sugar is needed in a formula to achieve acceptable results? That depends upon the desired outcome. If the criteria include having a product that is nutritionally acceptable, less sugar should be used than most recipes call for. The amount of sugar that can be eliminated before effects are noticeable varies from about one-fourth to one-third the original amount. Try taking a favorite formula and reducing the sugar by one-fourth, then one-third; in most cases, this results in a slightly less sweet but not markedly different baking product. If we truly are committed to baking healthier products, we must reduce the sugar in our formulas to moderate levels, as recommended by *The Dietary Guidelines*.

FATS

We eat too much total fat, saturated fat, and cholesterol for our own well-being. We should lower our intakes of these three if we are to live in good health. In baking, fat serves the following traditional purposes:

1. Imparts tenderness and flakiness
2. Aids in creaming and aerating
3. Adds flavor
4. Gives a perceived richness to products

How much fat is necessary to achieve the desired results? As with sugar, we must reduce the total amount we use to levels recommended by *The Dietary Guidelines*. Besides reducing the amount of fat, we need to consider the type of fat we use—whether it is saturated and how much cholesterol it contains (see Figure 6.2). Some fats, such as tropical oils and shortenings, are more saturated than vegetable margarines, while lard and butter contain

	Total fat (g)	Saturated fat (g)	Monosaturated fat (g)	Polyunsaturated fat (g)	Cholesterol (mg)
Canola oil	100	6	59	30	0
Safflower oil	100	9	12	74	0
Hard margarine	80	16	36	25	0
Soft margarine	61	13	32	13	0
Vegetable shortening (not-tropical)	100	25	45	26	0
Lard	100	39	45	11	95
Butter	81	51	23	3	219

FIGURE 6.2
Nutritional comparison of different types of fats per 100 grams (3.5 oz)

cholesterol. Soft margarines have less total fat than hard margarines and butter because they contain more water. Using soft margarines will reduce the total fat of our products even more, but the baking formula must be adjusted to account for the additional liquid in this type of margarine.

Remember fat has about nine Calories per gram, so it provides roughly twice as many Calories as either protein or carbohydrates. By reducing the fat content of bakery products, we can also reduce their Calorie content.

DAIRY PRODUCTS

Milk products are important ingredients in our bakery foods. Some of the benefits of adding milk to bakery products include improved crumb color and increased nutritional value. Fortunately, there is a wide variety of low-fat milk products available to the baker. You can use skim milk or nonfat milk solids instead of whole milk; yogurt or low-fat sour cream for regular sour cream; and low-fat buttermilk to impart tenderness to products without added fat. For a cream cheese substitute, try Neufchatel cheese, which has one-third less fat, or baker's cheese, which is virtually fat-free (see Figures 6.3 and 6.4).

Tofu, though not a dairy product, can nonetheless be substituted for cream cheese and eggs in certain recipes. Because it is vegetable-based, it has no cholesterol, and the fat it does contain is unsaturated (see Figure 6.5). For special dietary concerns such as lactose intolerance, tofu is an excellent substitute.

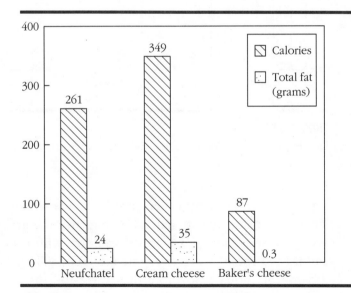

FIGURE 6.3
Calories and total fat per 100 grams (3.5 oz) of different types of soft cheeses

	Calories	Total fat (g)	Saturated fat (g)	Cholesterol (mg)
Whole milk	62	3.4	2	13.5
Skim milk	35	0.2	0.1	1.6
Buttermilk	40	0.9	0.5	3.7

FIGURE 6.4
Nutritional comparison per 100 grams (3.5 oz) of whole milk, skim milk, and buttermilk

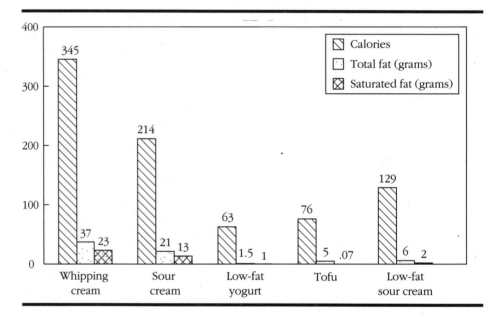

FIGURE 6.5
Calories, fat, and saturated fat per 100 grams (3.5 oz) of cream and substitutes

EGGS

Eggs are used in many bakery products, particularly in cookies and cakes. They give color, nutritional value, improve the grain and texture, add flavor, give structure, and increase volume. Unfortunately, whole eggs also add fat and cholesterol (see Figure 6.6). The yolk of one egg contains about 250 mg of cholesterol, more than three-fourths our daily allotment. It is essential, therefore, to limit the use of egg yolks in bakery products to reduce cholesterol amounts. One way to achieve this is to simply reduce the amount

	Whole egg	Egg white	Egg yolk
Fat (g)	10	0	31
Saturated fat (g)	3	0	9.5
Cholesterol (mg)	426	0	1283
Percentage of Calories from fat	62	0	79

FIGURE 6.6
Comparison of fat content of whole eggs, egg whites, and
egg yolks per 100 grams (3.5 oz)

of whole eggs used by at least one half, and add the remaining amount in
egg whites. For example, in a formula calling for two pounds of eggs, add
one pound of whole eggs and one pound of egg whites. Another approach
is to substitute all whites for the whole eggs, thereby totally eliminating the
cholesterol. Egg whites are available fresh, frozen, or dried.

For recipes in which eggs require no further cooking, as in a chiffon pie
filling, pasteurized eggs must be used to eliminate the dangers of salmonella
poisoning. Fresh eggs may be used if they are heated to 150° F before using.

There are a number of good egg substitutes on the market that may
work for particular formulas. If you decide to use one, be sure to check
its nutritional information to ensure that there is no added fat or egg yolk,
which would add cholesterol.

SALT

Salt plays an important role in breadmaking, the most essential one being
to control the action of the yeast. When making salt-free bread, the dough
must be given special attention so that it does not overproof. In cakes and
cookies, there is no real benefit in adding salt to any formula, but there is
a negative aspect—too much salt. According to *The Dietary Guidelines,* we
need to decrease our consumption of sodium. An easy way to accomplish
this is not to add salt to our sweet bakery products. By omitting the salt
from our typical formulas, sodium levels can be kept in line.

COCOA

Although cocoa is not an essential ingredient in baking, most bakeries make
some chocolate products, as they are very popular with customers. Since
its introduction into European cooking in the seventeenth century, choco-

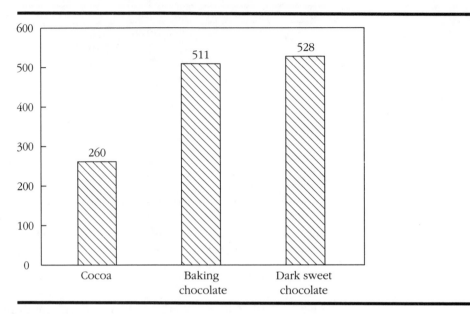

FIGURE 6.7
Calories per 100 grams (3.5 oz) of dark sweet chocolate, baking chocolate, and cocoa

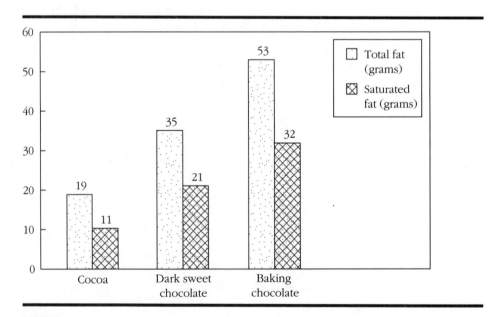

FIGURE 6.8
Grams of fat and saturated fat per 100 grams (3.5 oz) of cocoa, baking chocolate, and dark sweet chocolate

late consumption has steadily increased. There are two main sources for the chocolate used in baking: solid chocolate (baking and dark sweet) and cocoa. What are the nutritional differences between them? Specifically, baking chocolate and dark sweet chocolate have more fat, saturated fat, and Calories than cocoa (see Figures 6.7 and 6.8). When choosing a cocoa, bakers should select one that is 10 to 12 percent fat because some, such as the gourmet varieties, have twice as much fat. Cocoa is a better choice than solid chocolate because it has a lower fat content than solid chocolate. The formulas in this book use cocoa that is 12 percent fat. Delicious bakery products can be made with cocoa, and they will have lower fat and Calorie contents because of this minor substitution.

FRUITS AND NUTS

In addition to the main ingredients found in bakery products, other ingredients are used to add flavor, texture, color, nutritional value, and visual interest. These can include fruits and nuts. Fruits are excellent sources of vitamins and minerals, as well as being low in Calories, high in fiber, and virtually fat-free (see Figure 6.9). Two major drawbacks are their high price and their perishability. However, this should not deter bakers from using them, as they add many nutritional benefits.

Fruits are available fresh, frozen, canned, and dried. Fresh fruits are always a desirable ingredient for baked goods, because their flavor and quality greatly enhance the overall value. High-quality frozen and canned fruit offer similar positive characteristics.

	Calories	Fiber (g)	Fat (g)
Apples	59	2.5	0.4
Raspberries	49	6.2	0.5
Strawberries	30	2.6	0.4
Blueberries	57	2.7	0.4
Cranberries	48	4.2	0.2
Bananas	92	2.0	0.5
Raisins	300	5.9	0.5

FIGURE 6.9
Calories, fiber, and fat per 100 grams (3.5 oz) of various fruits

	Calories	Total fat (g)	Saturated fat (g)	Cholesterol (mg)	Percentage of Calories from fat
English walnuts	642	62	6	0	81
Almonds	589	52	5	0	74

FIGURE 6.10
Nutritional comparison of English walnuts and almonds

When we think of dried fruit, we generally picture raisins, dates, and prunes. But dried apricots, apples, and pears, to name a few, are also available. A variety of fruits adds both nutrition and eye appeal to bakery products.

Sugar-free fruit jams can also add to the aesthetic and nutritional value of bakery products. The jams recommended in the recipes in Part Two are sweetened with concentrated fruit juice but no added sugar or artificial sweeteners. These jams are indeed very sweet.

Nuts are another popular ingredient in bakery products. However, nuts are high in fat, albeit unsaturated (see Figure 6.10). Use nuts as part of the topping for cakes and cookies rather than as an ingredient added to the batter. Thus, fewer nuts are used, which avoids excess fat, but the perception of their flavor and texture remain.

FAT AND SUGAR SUBSTITUTES

FAT SUBSTITUTES

There are several fat replacements available to the food industry. These products provide the texturizing qualities of fat but are carbohydrate compounds, so they have from 1 Calorie per gram to 4 Calories per gram instead of the usual 9 Calories per gram from fat sources. Categorized as modified starches and gums, they provide a smooth, fat-like texture when used in fat-free baked goods (see Table 6.1). The difference in Calorie or fat content allows manufacturers to label these newly formulated products as "diet" or "low-fat" foods.

Recently, a protein-based fat substitute—Simplesse—received approval from the Food and Drug Administration. Simplesse is made from minute particles, by a process called *microparticulation,* of egg whites, milk proteins, or both. Because the particles are so small, the product is perceived by the tongue as a liquid. Simplesse can replace fat almost gram for gram, resulting in a decrease of 7 Calories per gram.

TABLE 6.1
Fat Substitutes

Carbohydrate-Based Fat Replacers

Cellulose (Avicel®cellulose gel)*
Various forms are used. One is a noncaloric purified form of cellulose ground to microparticles, which, when dispersed, form a network of particles with mouthfeel and flow properties similar to fat. Cellulose can replace some or all of the fat in dairy-type products, sauces, frozen desserts, and salad dressings.

Gums
Also called hydrophilic colloids or hydrocolloids. Examples include xanthan gum, guar gum, locust bean gum, gum arabic, and carrageenan. Virtually non-caloric; provide thickening, sometimes gelling effect; can promote creamy texture. Used in reduced-calorie, fat-free salad dressings and to reduce fat content in other formulated foods, including processed meats.

Dextrins (N-Oil®, Oatrim)
Four calorie per gram fat replacers that can replace some or all of the fat in a variety of products. Food sources for dextrins include tapioca and oat flour. Applications include salad dressings, puddings, spreads, dairy-type products, and frozen desserts.

Maltodextrins (Lycadex®, Maltrin®, Paselli SA2, STAR-DRI®)
Four calorie per gram gel or powder derived from carbohydrate sources such as corn, potato, wheat, and tapioca. Used as fat replacer, texture modifier, or bulking agent. Applications include baked goods, dairy products, salad dressings, spreads, sauces, frostings, fillings, processed meat, and frozen desserts.

Modified food starch (STA-SLIM™)
Four calorie per gram fat replacer, bodying agent, texture modifier. Can be derived from potato, corn, rice, wheat, or tapioca starches. Can be used together with emulsifiers, proteins, gums, and other modified food starches. Applications include processed meats, salad dressings, baked goods, fillings and frostings, sauces, condiments, frozen desserts, and dairy products.

Polydextrose (Litesse™)
Reduced-calorie (one calorie per gram) fat replacer and bulking agent. Water-soluble polymer of dextrose containing minor amounts of sorbitol and citric acid. Approved for use in variety of products, including baked goods, chewing gums, confections, salad dressings, frozen dairy desserts, gelatins, and puddings.

(continued)

*Brand names are shown in parentheses as examples.

Olestra is a fatty-acid based fat substitute currently under FDA review. Olestra is nonabsorbable and therefore noncaloric. If approved, it could be substituted for a percentage of the fat used in commercial deep-fat frying of snacks such as potato chips and in deep-fried bakery products.

SUGAR SUBSTITUTES

Even though we try to decrease our sugar and Calorie intake, we still seem to crave the sweet taste that sugar has. Sugar substitutes offer this sweetness with fewer Calories. The food industry has known this fact for a number of years, and have used sugar substitutes, most notably in soft drinks. There

TABLE 6.1
(*continued*)

Protein-Based Fat Replacers

Microparticulated Protein (Simplesse®)
Reduced-calorie (1 to 2 calories per gram)
ingredient made from cooking or blending
milk and egg protein. Digested as a protein.
Can be used in dairy-type products (e.g., ice
cream, butter, sour cream, cheese, yogurt),
as well as in salad dressing, margarine, and
mayonnaise-type products.

Other Protein Blends (Trailblazer®, ULTRA-
BAKE™, ULTRA-FREEZE™)
One example is a reduced-calorie fat substitute based on egg white and milk proteins.
Similar to micorparticulated protein but made
by a different process. Some blends of protein and carbohydrate can be used in frozen
desserts and baked goods.

Fat-Based Fat Replacers

Emulsifiers (Dur-Lo®, Veri-Lo™)
Examples include vegetable oil mono- and
diglyceride emulsifiers, which can, with water, replace all or part of the shortening content in cake mixes, cookies, icings, and numerous vegetable dairy products. Same caloric
value as fat (9 calories per gram) but less is
used, resulting in fat and calorie reduction.
In addition, emulsion systems using soybean
oil or milk fat can significantly reduce fat and
calories by replacing fat on a one-to-one basis.

Lipid (Fat/Oil) Analogs
■ **DDM****
Dialkyl dihexadecylmalonate (DDM) is a
non-caloric fatty alcohol ester of malonic and
alkylmalonic acids. Currently being developed
for high-temperature applications such as
chips, as well as mayonnaise- and margarine-
type products.

■ **Esterified Propoxylated Glycerol (EPG)****
Reuced-calorie fat replacer. May partially or
fully replace fats and oils in all typical consumer and commercial applications, including formulated products, baking, and frying.

■ **Sucrose Polyesters (Olestra)****
Calorie-free ingredient made from sucrose
and edible fats and oils. Not metabolized;
virtually unabsorbed by the body. May be
used in home cooking oils and shortenings,
and in commercial frying and snack foods.

■ **TATCA****
Trialkoxytricarballylate (TATCA)—tricarballylic
acid esterified with fatty alcohols under development for use in margarine- and mayonnaise-
type products. Has potential for other applications.

---

*Brand names are shown in parentheses as examples.
**Will require FDA approval.
Chart adapted with permission of the Calorie Control Council, Atlanta, Georgia.

are a variety of nutritive and non-nutritive sweeteners currently being used, and others awaiting FDA approval (see Table 6.2).

The nutritive sweetener Aspartame (called *NutraSweet* if a manufacturer adds it to a prepared product, or *Equal* if the consumer buys it plain for use as a table sweetener) is a protein, giving it the same number of Calories as sugar (4 per gram), but because it is 180 to 220 times as sweet as sugar, less is needed. However, aspartame loses its sweetness when exposed to cooking temperatures, making it impractical to use in baking, although it is used in frozen desserts.

TABLE 6.2
Nutritive and Non-nutritive Sweeteners

Sweetener	Derivation	Use	Manufacturer
Aspartame 180–200 times sweeter	Dipeptide (protein)	Puddings, gelatin desserts, beverage, table sweetener; loses sweetness when baked	NutraSweet Co. G.D. Searle Co.
Saccharin 300–400 times sweeter	Chemical production	Foods, beverages, drugs, table sweetener	
Acesulfame K 200 times sweeter	Acetoacetic acid	Gums, table sweetener, puddings	Hoechst AG. (a division of Hoechst Celanese Corporation)
Polydextrose About half as sweet	Many sugars	Replaces sugar as bulking agent	Pfizer, Inc.
Awaiting FDA Approval			
Sucralose 600 times sweeter	Sugar	Baked goods, mixes, beverages, frozen desserts, sauces	McNeil Specialty Products, Johnson & Johnson Co.
Alitame 2000 times sweeter	Amino acid (protein)	Baked goods, mixes, puddings	Pfizer, Inc.
Isomalt Half as sweet	Sugar alcohol	Candies, gums, frozen desserts, baked goods	Palatinit Süssungsmittel (Mannheim, Germany)

A nutritive sweetener called Isomalt may be approved soon. It is a sugar alcohol providing approximately 2 Calories per gram. Another low-calorie sweetener awaiting approval is Alitame, which is about 2000 times as sweet as sugar. Although using Alitame in baked products would decrease the Calorie content from sugar, it would increase the need for a bulking agent.

Acesulfame K (Sweet One) is the most recently approved non-nutritive sweetener. Its taste remains stable at baking temperatures, but it is approved only for home use as a table sweetener.

Saccharin is the oldest non-nutritive sweetener, discovered in 1879. The FDA and Congress will be reviewing its use in 1992. Until then, it can be found in most baked products labeled "dietetic."

Sucralose is a non-nutritive sweetener 600 times sweeter than sugar. The FDA is expected to approve it soon for use in frostings, baked goods, frozen dairy desserts, toppings, and mixes.

BULKING AGENTS

When a fat or sugar substitute is used, the volume of the product is affected. Low-Calorie bulking agents have been developed to provide the necessary

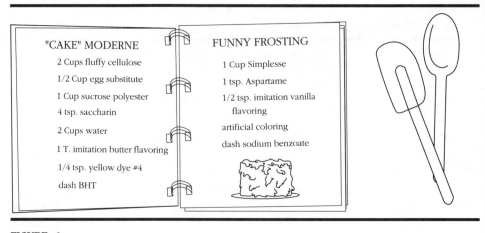

FIGURE 6.11
"Where's the flour?"

volume and moisture-giving properties of sugar and fat. Polydextrose, cellulose, and Isolmalt provide the texture for reduced-sugar and reduced-fat baked products.

**ACCEPTANCE AND
APPLICATION**

You could conclude that the production of low-Calorie baked goods is going to be a "piece of cake" with these products. However, using sugar and fat substitutes has many disadvantages. Choosing healthier foods is a serious issue. The addition of chemical substitutes in our bakery products is questionable in a number of ways (see Figure 6.11). Will customers accept a label that reads "... polydextrose, acesulfame K, olestra, isomalt..."? Also, these substitutes are expensive. The manufacturers have spent millions of dollars in the development, testing, and processing of these new ingredients. Can the small- to medium-volume baker really afford to utilize these substitutes? And, in the final analysis, do they really promote good health? Consumption of sugar substitutes has tripled since 1976, but unfortunately, this trend has not translated into reduced body weight. The sad truth is that more of us are overweight than ever before. Manufactured sugar and fat substitutes are not magic health pills. We need to carefully weigh all the consequences if we decide to use them in our bakery products.

COMPARATIVE NUTRITIONAL ANALYSES OF FORMULAS

An effective way to show how ingredient choices affect the nutritional aspect of products is to compare formulas side by side. We will look at two cake recipes to see how ingredient modifications can change the nutritional outcome in a positive way. We will compare each formula for the Calories, fat Calories, total fat, cholesterol, added grams of sugar, and percentage of Calories from fat (see Tables 6.3 and 6.4).

An important guideline to follow is the percentage of Calories derived from fat as opposed to carbohydrates and protein. The recommendation is that no more than 30 percent of our daily Caloric intake come from fats. The formula to figure this value is as follows:

$$\frac{\text{Grams of fat} \times 9 \text{ Calories/gram}}{\text{Total Calories}} \times 100 = \text{Percentage of Calories from fat}$$

However, we need to keep this in perspective, especially in relationship to baking formulas. The numbers are quite easy to misinterpret. For example, if one formula contains 5 grams of fat and has 125 Calories per serving, it derives 36 percent ($5 \times 9 = 45 \div 125 \times 100 = 36$ percent) of its Calories from fat, more than the recommended 30 percent. Another formula has 10 grams of fat and 350 Calories per serving, which means that about 26 percent ($10 \times 9 = 90 \div 350 \times 100 = 26$ percent) of its Calories come from fat, a figure within the recommended 30 percent. Does that make it a better product than the first? Definitely not, since it has twice as many grams of fat as the first formula. Nevertheless, foods with fat percentages over 30 percent should be consumed less often. Be wary of the percentage game, and always check the total fat amount, as it is a better indicator of a healthful product.

HEALTHFUL SUBSTITUTIONS AND MODIFICATIONS

Products such as skim milk, low-fat sour cream, yogurt, and egg substitutes made from egg whites can help a baker achieve the healthful alternative his or her customers are seeking. Reformulating a favorite recipe to a lower-sugar, lower-fat version takes time and effort. However, reducing the sugar and fat and adding fiber or juice allows you to list known ingredients on the label—ones that customers will be able to understand.

You should try these tested formulas that use products already familiar to your customers. The recipes in this text have been reformulated using less fat and sugar. Customers may discover "new" healthful favorites without the added concern over chemicals and increased cost.

Table 6.5 offers a list of common ingredients and substitutes for producing healthier baked goods.

TABLE 6.3
Formula Comparison: Pound Cake (2 Ounce Serving Size)

Standard Formula			Formula from This Text		
Sugar	2 lb		Sugar	1 lb	4oz
Vegetable shortening	1 lb	4 oz	*Margarine*	1 lb	
Whole eggs	1 lb	4 oz	*Egg whites*		12 oz
Cake flour	2 lb		Cake flour	2 lb	6 oz
Baking powder		½ oz	*Baking soda*		½ oz
Salt		¼ oz	Salt	none	
Whole milk	1 lb		*Lowfat yogurt*	2 lb	

Nutritional Analysis

Calories	214	168
Fat calories	99	54
Total fat	11 g	6 g
Cholesterol	40 mg	1 mg
Added sugars	15 g	9 g
Percentage of calories from fat	**46%**	**32%**

TABLE 6.4
Formula Comparison: Carrot Cake (3 Ounce Serving Size—Without Icing)

Standard Formula			Formula from This Text		
Pastry flour		14 oz	Pastry flour		14 oz
			Whole wheat flour		6 oz
Baking soda		½ oz	Baking soda		1 oz
Salt		2 tsp	Salt		
White sugar	1 lb	8 oz	*Brown sugar*		12 oz
Oil		14 oz	Oil		3 oz
Whole eggs		12 oz	Whole eggs		4 oz
			Egg whites		5 oz
Carrots	1 lb	4 oz	Carrots	1 lb	6 oz
			Buttermilk		11 oz
Pineapple		14 oz	Pineapple	1 lb	
Coconut		2 oz	*Raisins*		5 oz

Nutritional Analysis

Calories	262	169
Fat calories	99	27
Total fat	14 g	3 g
Cholesterol	39 mg	15 mg
Added sugars	21 g	11 g
Percentage of calories from fat	**38%**	**16%**

TABLE 6.5
Healthful Ingredient Substitutions and Modifications

Ingredient	Substitution	Nutritional Benefits
White bread flour	Part or all whole wheat flour, other whole-grain flours—rye, buckwheat, oat, triticale, amaranth, corn	Increased fiber, vitamins, minerals
White pastry flour	Part or all whole-wheat pastry flour, or other whole-grain flour	Increased fiber, vitamins, minerals
Butter or lard	Vegetable margarines	No cholesterol
Tropical oils	Vegetable oils such as canola and safflower	Less saturated fat
Whole milk	Skim milk, buttermilk	Less total fat, saturated fat, and cholesterol, fewer calories
Cream cheese	Baker's cheese, Neufchatel cheese	Less total fat, saturated fat, and cholesterol, fewer calories
Sour cream	Reduced-fat sour cream	Less total fat and saturated fat, fewer calories
Cream	Lowfat yogurt, tofu	Less total fat and saturated fat, fewer calories, no cholesterol with tofu
Whole eggs	Egg whites	No cholesterol or fat, fewer calories
	Egg substitutes	Less total fat, cholesterol
Baking chocolate	Cocoa	Less fat and saturated fat, fewer calories

Other modifications:
For total fat in formula, use half fat and half unsweetened applesauce.

Reduce the fat called for by one-fourth to one-third the original amount.

Reduce the sugar called for by one-fouth to one-third the orginal amount.

To reduce sodium content, omit salt from all sweet bakery products.

To replace some or all of the sugar, add fruit concentrates (they should be 100% real fruit juice). Reduce liquid accordingly, increase baking soda, and decrease baking powder.

Increase the fiber content of a product by adding fruit.

BIBLIOGRAPHY

Pennington, Jean A. T., and Helen Nichols Church. *Food Values of Portions Commonly Used.* 15th rev. ed. New York: Harper and Row, Publishers, 1989.

Pyler, E. J. *Baking Science and Technology.* Vol. I, 3d rev. ed, Merriam, Kansas: Sosland Publishing Company, 1988.

ACTIVITY

Review this formula. What adjustments (ingredient substitutions or modifications) could you make so it would be more nutritious?

Banana Cake

Standard Formula			Revised Formula
Cake flour	1 lb	4 oz	
Sugar	1 lb	8 oz	
Salt		¾ oz	
Baking powder		¾ oz	
Baking soda		¼ oz	
Shortening		8 oz	
Bananas	1 lb		
Whole milk		8 oz	
Whole eggs	1 lb		
Vanilla		½ oz	

101 HEALTHFUL BAKING FORMULAS

Please read these few words on the formulas before you begin. For the nutritional information to be accurate, you cannot substitute any of the ingredients. However, do not let that stop you from experimenting with, for example, different flours or fruits from those called for in a formula. The nutritional information will vary somewhat, but you will still have a nutritionally acceptable product.

Most ingredients should be at room temperature before you begin, with the exception of a few. When used for pastry making, margarine should be well chilled before it is added to the flour. Because of the increased potential of salmonella contamination, eggs should be kept refrigerated until ready to use, then brought to room temperature quickly over warm water.

The procedures for mixing and baking follow standard baking techniques. One difference occurs in some of the directions for creaming ingredients. Since the formulas in this book have very little fat, some of them call for a portion of the eggs or egg whites to be added in order to cream the fat and sugar together. When a formula calls for a lightly greased pan, it means just that—*lightly* greased. You can use either a light mist of pan-release spray or a very thin coating of pan grease. Anything heavier than that will make the nutritional information incorrect. In order to keep the nutritional information as accurate as possible, be very careful when weighing out ingredients. In addition, it's very important to adhere to the portions listed with each formula. Cut bars and cakes into the exact number of portions, no more or less.

The finished products may seem slightly different to you at first. We started with standard formulas and modified them to incorporate the healthier baking principles discussed in this text. Products made with whole-grain flours, for instance, will, because of their increased fiber content, be slightly heavier and denser in texture, than those made with only white flour. This in no way detracts from the taste quality. In fact, whole grains impart a unique and delicious flavor. We reduced the sugars in the formulas to levels that we believe are more conducive to good health. Most of you will never notice the reduction, and those who do will soon become accustomed to the less sweet taste. A much easier change was reducing the sodium levels in these recipes. With the exception of the yeast breads and rolls, we simply eliminated the added salt from the recipes. To reduce the sodium level further, use reduced-sodium baking powder, baking soda, and unsalted margarine. In some ways, reducing the fat in these formulas was the hardest modification. Less fat can mean a drier-textured product, shorter shelf life, and less flavor. By adding other moisture-giving ingredients, however, such as buttermilk, applesauce, and other liquids, we have successfully avoided those pitfalls.

7 YEAST BREADS AND ROLLS

Bread is good for you! Compared to many foods, bread is low in total fat, cholesterol, and calories, and, if it contains whole grains, it becomes an excellent source of complex carbohydrates and fiber. Breads are also delicious and satisfying. You can make an endless variety of breads by substituting and adding different flours, grains, and even fruits and vegetables. Don't limit yourself to the formulas here. Experiment and discover what interesting and tasty breads and rolls you can create by modifying and substituting ingredients to create a more healthful product.

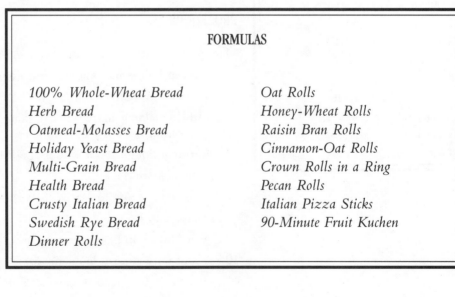

FORMULAS

100% Whole-Wheat Bread
Herb Bread
Oatmeal-Molasses Bread
Holiday Yeast Bread
Multi-Grain Bread
Health Bread
Crusty Italian Bread
Swedish Rye Bread
Dinner Rolls

Oat Rolls
Honey-Wheat Rolls
Raisin Bran Rolls
Cinnamon-Oat Rolls
Crown Rolls in a Ring
Pecan Rolls
Italian Pizza Sticks
90-Minute Fruit Kuchen

100% WHOLE-WHEAT BREAD

YIELD: 10 loaves, 1 lb (450 g) each
PORTIONS: 80
PORTION SIZE: 2 oz (57 g)

Nutritional Information per Serving		
	Amount	Calories
Calories		133
Fat	1 g	9
Saturated fatty acid	< 1 g	1
Cholesterol	< 1 mg	
Carbohydrate	27 g	
Added sugars	1 g	
Fiber	4.5 g	
Protein	5 g	
Sodium	282 mg	
Potassium	177 mg	
Vitamin A	10 RE	
Vitamin C	<1 mg	
Calcium	32 mg	
Iron	1 mg	

4 lb		Water, warm, 105° F (41° C)	1800 g
	2 oz	Yeast, dry	55 g
	4 oz	Honey	110 g
3 lb		Whole wheat flour	1360 g
	2 oz	Oil	55 g
	4 oz	Nonfat milk solids	110 g
	2 oz	Salt	55 g
3 lb	4 oz	Whole wheat flour	1470 g
11 lb	2 oz	Total weight	5015 g

PROCEDURE

1. Add yeast to warm water; let stand 5 minutes.
2. Mix in honey and whole wheat flour.
3. Ferment 30 minutes. Stir down.
4. Add remaining ingredients, mixing on second speed of 3- or 4-speed mixer, for 7 to 8 minutes.
5. Ferment dough about 1 hour at 80° F (27° C) or until doubled.
6. Punch down dough.
7. Scale dough into ten 18 oz (510 g) pieces.
8. Shape into loaves.
9. Place loaves in lightly greased bread pans.
10. Proof until almost double in size.
11. Bake at 360° F (180° C) about 25 minutes or until done.

HERB BREAD

YIELD:	10 loaves, 1 lb (450 g) each
PORTIONS:	80
PORTION SIZE:	2 oz (57 g)

Nutritional Information per Serving		
	Amount	Calories
Calories		146
Fat	2 g	18
Saturated fatty acid	<1 g	1
Cholesterol	<1 mg	
Carbohydrate	23 g	
Added sugars	1 g	
Fiber	2 g	
Protein	5 g	
Sodium	296 mg	
Potassium	141 mg	
Vitamin A	28 RE	
Vitamin C	<1 mg	
Calcium	56 mg	
Iron	2 mg	

4 lb		Water, warm, 105° F (41° C)	1800 g
	2 oz	Yeast, dry	55 g
	3 oz	Sugar	85 g
	2 oz	Salt	55 g
	10 oz	Nonfat milk solids	280 g
	3 oz	Oil	85 g
4 lb	4 oz	Bread flour	1900 g
1 lb	8 oz	Whole wheat flour	680 g
	1 oz	Parsley, fresh chopped	30 g
	1½ tsp	Oregano, dried	3 g
	2 tsp	Chives, dried	1 g
	¼ oz	Basil, dried	6 g
11 lb	2 oz	Total weight	4980 g

PROCEDURE

1. Add yeast to warm water; let stand 5 minutes.
2. Add remaining ingredients, mixing on second speed for 7 to 8 minutes.
3. Ferment dough about 1 hour at 80° F (27° C) or until doubled.
4. Punch down dough.
5. Scale dough into ten 18 oz (510 g) pieces.
6. Shape into loaves.
7. Place loaves in lightly greased bread pans.
8. Proof until double in size.
9. Bake at 360° F (180° C) about 25 minutes or until done.

OATMEAL-MOLASSES BREAD

YIELD: 11 loaves, 1 lb (450 g) each
PORTIONS: 88
PORTION SIZE: 2 oz (57 g)

Nutritional Information per Serving		
	Amount	*Calories*
Calories		151
Fat	2 g	18
Saturated fatty acid	<1 g	2
Cholesterol	11 mg	
Carbohydrate	28 g	
Added sugars	4 g	
Fiber	3 g	
Protein	5 g	
Sodium	256 mg	
Potassium	137 mg	
Vitamin A	6 RE	
Vitamin C	0 mg	
Calcium	20 mg	
Iron	2 mg	

3 lb		Water, boiling	1350 g
1 lb		Oats, quick	450 g
	12 oz	Molasses	340 g
	4 oz	Oil	110 g
	2 oz	Salt	55 g
1 lb		Water, warm, 105° F (41° C)	450 g
	2 oz	Yeast, dry	55 g
	8 oz	Eggs	230 g
3 lb	8 oz	Bread flour	1600 g
2 lb	4 oz	Whole wheat flour	1020 g
	4 oz	Oats, quick	110 g
12 lb	12 oz	Total weight	5770 g

PROCEDURE

1. Combine boiling water, oats, molasses, oil, and salt. Cool to 105° F (38° C).

2. Add yeast to warm water; let stand 5 minutes. Stir into oat mixture.

3. Add remaining ingredients, except last 4 oz (110 g) oats, mixing on second speed for 7 to 8 minutes.

4. Ferment dough about 1 hour at 80° F (27° C), or until doubled.

5. Punch down dough.

6. Scale dough into eleven 18 oz (510 g) pieces.

7. Shape into loaves. Brush loaves with egg wash, then roll in 4 oz oats.

8. Place loaves in lightly greased bread pans.

9. Proof until doubled in size.

10. Bake at 360° F (180° C) about 25 to 30 minutes or until done.

Egg Wash

2 oz	Eggs	55 g
3 oz	Water	85 g

Beat together.

HOLIDAY YEAST BREAD

YIELD: 12 loaves, 1 lb (450 g) each
PORTIONS: 96
PORTION SIZE: 2.5 oz (72 g)

		Nutritional Information per Serving	

	Amount	Calories
Calories		196
Fat	3 g	27
Saturated fatty acid	<1 g	5
Cholesterol	20 mg	
Carbohydrate	38 g	
Added sugars	9 g	
Fiber	2 g	
Protein	5 g	
Sodium	158 mg	
Potassium	129 mg	
Vitamin A	41 RE	
Vitamin C	<1 mg	
Calcium	31 mg	
Iron	2 mg	

		Ingredient	
2 lb	12 oz	Water, warm, 105° F (41° C)	1250 g
	3 oz	Yeast, dry	85 g
	2 oz	Sugar	55 g
1 lb		Bread flour	450 g
	12 oz	Whole wheat flour	340 g
	8 oz	Sugar	230 g
	8 oz	Margarine, unsalted, room temperature	230 g
	4 oz	Nonfat milk solids	110 g
	1½ oz	Salt	43 g
1 lb		Eggs	450 g
	2 oz	Vanilla	55 g
	1 oz	Lemon rind	28 g
4 lb	8 oz	Bread flour	2000 g
	12 oz	Currants	340 g
	6 oz	Mixed glacé fruit	170 g
13 lb		Total weight	5836 g

PROCEDURE

1. Add yeast to warm water; let stand 5 minutes.
2. Mix in sugar, 1 lb (450 g) bread flour, and whole wheat flour.
3. Ferment 30 minutes. Stir down.
4. Add remaining ingredients, mixing on second speed for 7 to 8 minutes.
5. Ferment dough about 1 hour at 80° F (27° C) or until doubled.
6. Punch down dough.
7. Scale dough into twelve 18 oz (510 g) pieces.
8. Form into stollen or loaf shapes.
9. Place loaves in lightly greased bread pans or on parchment-lined sheet pans.
10. Proof until almost double in size.

11.   Bake at 350° F (175° C) about 25 minutes or until done.

12.   Immediately brush with glaze. Cool. Ice.

Glaze

3 oz	Sugar	85 g
3 oz	Water	85 g

Bring to a rolling boil.

Icing

1 lb	Confectioners' sugar	450 g
3 oz	Corn syrup	85 g
3 oz	Water	85 g
½ oz	Vanilla	14 g

Mix until smooth. Heat to 100° F (38° C) before using.

MULTI-GRAIN BREAD

YIELD:	11 loaves, 1 lb (450 g) each
PORTIONS:	88 servings
PORTION SIZE:	2 oz (57 g)

3 lb		Water, boiling	1360 g
2 lb		Six- or seven-grain hot cereal	900 g
1 lb		Water, warm, 105° F (41° C)	450 g
	3 oz	Yeast, dry	85 g
	6 oz	Honey	170 g
	2 oz	Salt	55 g
4 lb		Bread flour	1800 g
1 lb	6 oz	Whole wheat flour	620 g
	5 oz	Oil	140 g
12 lb	6 oz	Total weight	5580 g

Nutritional Information per Serving

	Amount	Calories
Calories		153
Fat	2 g	18
Saturated fatty acid	<1 g	1
Cholesterol	0 mg	
Carbohydrate	30 g	
Added sugars	2 g	
Fiber	4 g	
Protein	5 g	
Sodium	252 mg	
Potassium	71 mg	
Vitamin A	<1 RE	
Vitamin C	<1 mg	
Calcium	11 mg	
Iron	2 mg	

PROCEDURE

1. Combine boiling water and cereal. Cool to 105° F (38° C).

2. Add yeast to warm water; let stand 5 minutes. Stir into cereal mixture.

3. Add remaining ingredients, mixing on second speed for 7 to 8 minutes.

4. Ferment dough about 1 hour at 80° F (27° C) or until doubled.

5. Punch down dough.

6. Scale dough into eleven 18 oz (510 g) pieces.

7. Shape into loaves.

8. Place loaves in lightly greased bread pans.

9. Proof until almost double in size.

10. Bake at 360° F (180° C) about 25 to 30 minutes or until done.

HEALTH BREAD

YIELD: 9 loaves, 1 lb 8 oz (680 g) each
PORTIONS: 112
PORTION SIZE: 2 oz (57 g)

Nutritional Information per Serving

	Amount	Calories
Calories		138
Fat	1 g	9
Saturated fatty acid	<1 g	
Cholesterol	0 mg	
Carbohydrate	21 g	
Added sugars	3 g	
Fiber	1 g	
Protein	11 g	
Sodium	158 mg	
Potassium	110 mg	
Vitamin A	10 RE	
Vitamin C	1 mg	
Calcium	21 mg	
Iron	1 mg	

8 oz	Water, warm, 105° F (41° C)	240 g
2 oz	Yeast, dry	60 g
8 oz	Oatmeal	230 g
2 oz	Shortening	60 g
1½ oz	Salt	40 g
1 lb	Raisins, dark	450 g
4 lb	Water, boiling	1810 g
3 oz	Bran cereal buds	85 g
10 oz	Molasses, light	280 g
1 lb	Whole wheat flour	450 g
6 lb	Bread flour	2720 g
14 lb	Total weight	6425 g

PROCEDURE

1. Add yeast to warm water; let stand 5 minutes.
2. In a large bowl, combine next six ingredients; cool.
3. Stir in softened yeast and molasses.
4. Add flours and mix 10 minutes at second speed.
5. Let rise about 1½ hours at 80° F (27° C) or until double.
6. Punch down dough.
7. Scale into nine 25 oz (710 g) pieces.
8. Shape into loaves.
9. Place loaves in lightly greased bread pans.
10. Proof until almost double in size.
11. Bake at 400° F (200° C) about 60 minutes or until done.

CRUSTY ITALIAN BREAD

YIELD:	9 lb (4056 g)
PORTIONS:	72 rolls, or 144 bread sticks, or 6 loaves
PORTION SIZE:	2 oz (57 g) roll or bread slice or 1 oz (28 g) bread stick

3 lb	8 oz	Water, warm, 105° F (41° c)	1580 g
	2 oz	Yeast, dry	56 g
	2 oz	Sugar	56 g
	1½ oz	Salt	44 g
	3½ oz	Olive oil	100 g
4 lb	4 oz	Bread flour	1820 g
	14 oz	Egg whites, stiffly beaten	400 g
9 lb	3 oz	Total weight	4056 g

PROCEDURE

1. Add yeast to warm water; let stand 5 minutes.

2. Add sugar, salt, oil, and 1½ lb (680 g) flour.

3. Beat well with mixer at second speed.

4. Fold beaten egg whites into batter.

5. Add remaining flour, mixing at second speed about 10 minutes.

6. Ferment dough about 1 hour at 80° F (27° C) or until double.

7. Punch down dough.

8. Let dough ferment for one more hour at 80° F (27° C).

9. Punch down dough and form into desired shape.

10. Place rolls, loaves, or sticks on lightly greased baking sheets that are sprinkled lightly with cornmeal.

11. Brush with egg wash.

12. Proof at 90° F (32° C) until double in size, about 30 minutes.

13. Place a large shallow pan of boiling water on the bottom rack of the oven to provide steam while the bread bakes. Bake at 425° F (220° C) until brown and crusty, about 20 minutes. Watch bread sticks carefully.

Nutritional Information per Serving

	Amount	Calories
Calories		121
Fat	2 g	18
Saturated fatty acid	0 g	
Cholesterol	0 mg	
Carbohydrate	14 g	
Added sugars	1 g	
Fiber	<1 g	
Protein	12 g	
Sodium	238 mg	
Potassium	39 mg	
Vitamin A	<1 mg	
Vitamin C	0 mg	
Calcium	13 mg	
Iron	<1 mg	

Note: Nutritional information for bread sticks would be one-half the amount for the roll and bread slice.

SHAPING FOR LOAVES

1. Scale dough into six 24 oz (680 g) pieces.
2. Flatten dough with hands.
3. Roll up tightly, sealing the seam well.
4. Using the palms of the hands, roll the loaf on the bench until the loaf is oval-shaped. The ends should be tapered but not pointed.
5. Place seam-side down on prepared baking sheets.
6. Brush with egg wash.
7. Slash with a very sharp knife, making diagonal cuts along the top.

SHAPING FOR ROLLS

1. Scale dough into seventy-two 2 oz (57 g) pieces. Round up.
2. Place on prepared baking sheet.
3. Brush with egg wash.
4. Slash the top with a very sharp knife.

SHAPING FOR BREAD STICKS

1. Scale dough into six 24 oz (680 g) pieces.
2. Roll out each portion to a rectangle, 12 × 7 in (30 × 17 cm).
3. Cut each rectangle into twenty-four ½ in (1 cm) strips.
4. Roll strips to 8 in (20 cm) in length.
5. Place on prepared baking sheet, 1 in (2½ cm) apart.
6. Brush with egg wash.

Egg Wash

| 1½ oz | Egg whites | 44 g |
| 2 oz | Water | 56 g |

Beat together.

SWEDISH RYE BREAD

YIELD:	4 loaves, 1½ lb (675 g) each
PORTIONS:	48
PORTION SIZE:	2 oz (57 g)

Nutritional Information per Serving		
	Amount	Calories
Calories		148
Fat	2 g	18
Saturated fatty acid	0 g	
Cholesterol	0 mg	
Carbohydrate	23 g	
Added sugars	5 g	
Fiber	1 g	
Protein	11 g	
Sodium	222 mg	
Potassium	87 mg	
Vitamin A	0 RE	
Vitamin C	1 mg	
Calcium	22 mg	
Iron	1 mg	

1 lb	12 oz	Water, warm, 105° F (41° C)	795 g
	¾ oz	Yeast, dry	21 g
	3¾ oz	Brown sugar	110 g
	5½ oz	Molasses, light	160 g
	1 oz	Salt	28 g
	2 oz	Oil	60 g
1 lb	8 oz	Water, hot	680 g
1 lb	4 oz	Rye flour, medium	570 g
	¾ oz	Orange peel, grated	24 g
2 lb	8 oz	Bread flour	1136 g
6 lb	9 oz	Total weight	3013 g

PROCEDURE

1. Add yeast to warm water; let stand 5 minutes.
2. Combine the sugar, molasses, salt, oil, water, rye flour, and orange peel in a large bowl and mix well.
3. Add the dissolved yeast.
4. Add bread flour.
5. Mix at least 5 minutes to make a smooth dough.
6. Ferment dough 1½ hours at 78° F (26° C) or until doubled.
7. Punch down dough.
8. Shape into four 26 oz (728 g) pieces.
9. Cover and let rest for 10 minutes.
10. Shape into round loaves.
11. Place on lightly greased baking sheet.
12. Proof until almost double in size.
13. Bake at 375° F (190° C) about 25 to 30 minutes or until done.

DINNER ROLLS

YIELD: **12 dozen**
PORTIONS: **144**
PORTION SIZE: **1½ oz (43 g) roll**

	Nutritional Information per Serving	
	Amount	Calories
Calories		112
Fat	2 g	18
Saturated fatty acid	<1 g	8
Cholesterol	4 mg	
Carbohydrate	20 g	
Added sugars	2 g	
Fiber	1 g	
Protein	3 g	
Sodium	183 mg	
Potassium	62 mg	
Vitamin A	23 RE	
Vitamin C	<1 mg	
Calcium	23 mg	
Iron	1 mg	

4 lb		Water, warm, 105° F (41° C)	1800 g
	3 oz	Yeast, dry	85 g
	8 oz	Sugar	230 g
	8 oz	Margarine, unsalted, room temperature	230 g
	6 oz	Nonfat milk solids	170 g
	2 oz	Salt	55 g
7 lb	9 oz	Bread flour	3500 g
13 lb	4 oz	Total weight	6070 g

PROCEDURE

1. Add yeast to warm water; let stand 5 minutes.
2. Add remaining ingredients, mixing on second speed for 7 to 8 minutes.
3. Ferment dough about 1 hour at 80° F (27° C) or until doubled.
4. Punch down dough.
5. Scale dough into four 3 lb 6 oz (1470 g) pieces.
6. Round up in bun divider.
7. Place rolls on parchment-lined baking sheets. Brush with egg wash.
8. Proof until double in size.
9. Bake at 375° F (190° C) for 15 to 18 minutes or until golden brown.

Egg Wash

2 oz	Eggs	55 g
3 oz	Water	85 g

Beat together.

OAT ROLLS

YIELD:	9 dozen
PORTIONS:	108
PORTION SIZE:	1¾ oz (50 g) roll

Nutritional Information per Serving		
	Amount	Calories
Calories		120
Fat	2 g	18
Saturated fatty acid	<1 g	1
Cholesterol	5 mg	
Carbohydrate	23 g	
Added sugars	3 g	
Fiber	2 g	
Protein	4 g	
Sodium	212 mg	
Potassium	97 mg	
Vitamin A	11 RE	
Vitamin C	<1 mg	
Calcium	23 mg	
Iron	1 mg	

4 lb		Water, warm, 105° F (41° C)	1800 g
	3 oz	Yeast, dry	85 g
	8 oz	Sugar	230 g
	2 oz	Molasses	55 g
2 lb		Whole wheat flour	900 g
	8 oz	Oats, quick	230 g
	8 oz	Cornmeal	230 g
	4 oz	Oil	110 g
	4 oz	Nonfat milk solids	110 g
	4 oz	Eggs	110 g
	2 oz	Salt	55 g
3 lb	5 oz	Bread flour	1500 g
	4 oz	Oats, quick	110 g
12 lb	4 oz	Total weight	5525 g

PROCEDURE

1. Add yeast to warm water; let stand 5 minutes.
2. Mix in sugar, molasses, whole wheat flour, oats, and cornmeal.
3. Ferment 30 minutes. Stir down.
4. Add remaining ingredients, except last 4 oz (110 g) oats, mixing on second speed for 7 to 8 minutes.
5. Ferment dough about 1 hour at 80° F (27° C) or until doubled.
6. Punch down dough.
7. Scale dough into three 4 lb (1800 g) pieces.
8. Round up in bun divider.
9. Place rolls on parchment-lined baking sheets. Brush with egg wash, and dip tops in oats.
10. Proof until double in size.
11. Bake at 375° F (190° C) for 15 to 18 minutes or until golden brown.

Egg Wash

| 2 oz | Eggs | 55 g |
| 3 oz | Water | 85 g |

Beat together.

HONEY-WHEAT ROLLS

YIELD: 9 dozen
PORTIONS: 108
PORTION SIZE: 1¾ oz (50 g) roll

Nutritional Information per Serving		
	Amount	*Calories*
Calories		115
Fat	2 g	18
Saturated fatty acid	<1 g	1
Cholesterol	5 mg	
Carbohydrate	22 g	
Added sugars	2 g	
Fiber	2 g	
Protein	4 g	
Sodium	212 mg	
Potassium	99 mg	
Vitamin A	10 RE	
Vitamin C	<1 mg	
Calcium	22 mg	
Iron	1 mg	

4 lb		Water, warm, 105° F (41° C)	1800 g
	3 oz	Yeast, dry	85 g
	8 oz	Honey	230 g
3 lb	8 oz	Whole wheat flour	1600 g
	4 oz	Oil	110 g
	4 oz	Nonfat milk solids	110 g
	4 oz	Eggs	110 g
	2 oz	Salt	55 g
3 lb		Bread flour	1350 g
12 lb	1 oz	Total weight	5450 g

PROCEDURE

1. Add yeast to warm water; let stand 5 minutes.
2. Mix in honey and whole wheat flour.
3. Ferment 30 minutes. Stir down.
4. Add remaining ingredients, mixing on second speed for 7 to 8 minutes.
5. Ferment dough about 1 hour at 80° F (27° C) or until doubled.
6. Punch down dough.
7. Scale dough into three 4 lb (1800 g) pieces.
8. Round up in bun divider.
9. Place rolls on parchment-lined baking sheets. Brush with egg wash.
10. Proof until double in size.
11. Bake at 375° F (190° C) for 15 to 18 minutes or until golden brown.

Egg Wash

2 oz	Eggs	55 g
3 oz	Water	85 g

Beat together.

RAISIN BRAN ROLLS

YIELD:	8 dozen	
PORTIONS:	96	
PORTION SIZE:	2½ oz (72 g) roll	

Nutritional Information per Serving		
	Amount	*Calories*
Calories		185
Fat	3 g	27
Saturated fatty acid	<1 g	5
Cholesterol	20 mg	
Carbohydrate	35 g	
Added sugars	10 g	
Fiber	2 g	
Protein	5 g	
Sodium	192 mg	
Potassium	135 mg	
Vitamin A	41 RE	
Vitamin C	<1 mg	
Calcium	29 mg	
Iron	2 mg	

2 lb	12 oz	Water, warm, 105° F (41° C)	1250 g
	3 oz	Yeast, dry	85 g
	3 oz	Sugar	85 g
1 lb		Bread flour	450 g
	12 oz	Whole wheat flour	340 g
	8 oz	Sugar	230 g
	8 oz	Margarine, unsalted, room temperature	230 g
	4 oz	Nonfat milk solids	110 g
	1½ oz	Salt	43 g
1 lb		Eggs	450 g
	2 oz	Vanilla	55 g
4 lb	4 oz	Bread flour	1920 g
11 lb	10 oz	Total weight	5248 g

PROCEDURE

1. Add yeast to warm water; let stand 5 minutes.

2. Mix in sugar, 1 lb (450 g) bread flour, and whole wheat flour.

3. Ferment 30 minutes. Stir down.

4. Add remaining ingredients, mixing on second speed for 7 to 8 minutes.

5. Ferment dough about 1 hour at 80° F (27° C) or until doubled.

6. Punch down dough.

7. Roll out dough into a rectangle.

8. Spread bran smear over dough. Sprinkle with raisins.

9. Roll up dough, jelly-roll style. Seal edge.

10. Cut into 96 rolls, 2½ oz (65 g) each. Place on parchment-lined sheets.

11. Proof until double in size.

12. Bake at 375° F (190° C) for 15 to 18 minutes or until golden brown.

13. Ice when cool.

Egg Wash

2 oz	Eggs	55 g
3 oz	Water	85 g

Beat together.

Bran Smear

10 oz	Egg whites		280 g
5 oz	Wheat bran		140 g
5 oz	Sugar		140 g
¼ oz	Cinnamon		7 g
4 oz	Water		110 g
12 oz	Raisins		340 g
2 lb 4 oz	Total weight		1017 g

Beat all ingredients except raisins to a smooth paste.

Icing

1 lb 2 oz	Confectioners' sugar	510 g
3 oz	Corn syrup	85 g
3 oz	Water	85 g

Mix until smooth. Heat to 100° F (38° C) before using.

CINNAMON-OAT ROLLS

YIELD: 7 dozen
PORTIONS: 84
PORTION SIZE: 2½ oz (70 g) roll

Nutritional Information per Serving		
	Amount	*Calories*
Calories		182
Fat	5 g	45
Saturated fatty acid	1 g	9
Cholesterol	24 mg	
Carbohydrate	23 g	
Added sugars	10 g	
Fiber	1 g	
Protein	11 g	
Sodium	184 g	
Potassium	85 g	
Vitamin A	65 RE	
Vitamin C	<1 mg	
Calcium	39 mg	
Iron	<1 mg	

3 lb		Skim milk, scalded	1375 g
	12 oz	Oat bran	340 g
1 lb	15 oz	Water, warm, 105° F (41° C)	885 g
	3 oz	Yeast, dry	85 g
	14 oz	Eggs	400 g
	11½ oz	Margarine, softened	330 g
	10½ oz	Sugar	300 g
	1 oz	Salt	28 g
	8 oz	Bread flour	225 g
3 lb	8 oz	Bread flour	1600 g
	4 oz	Margarine, melted	113 g
	10 oz	Sugar	285 g
	1 oz	Cinnamon	28 g
13 lb	2 oz	Total weight	5994 g

PROCEDURE

1. Mix scalded milk with oat bran. Cool.

2. In large mixing bowl, dissolve yeast in warm water. Add to milk mixture.

3. Add eggs, margarine, sugar, salt, and 8 oz (225 g) flour. Mix until smooth.

4. Add enough remaining flour to make a soft dough.

5. Mix dough on second speed for four minutes.

6. Ferment dough about 1½ hours at 80° F (27° C) or until doubled.

7. Scale into two 6 lb (2.7 kg) pieces.

8. Roll each piece into a rectangle about ¼ inch thick.

9. Brush each piece with ½ oz (14 g) melted butter.

10. Sprinkle each piece with 1½ oz (40 g) sugar and 1 tsp cinnamon.

11. Roll up jelly-roll fashion.

12. Cut into 2½ oz (70 g) rolls.

13. Place cut side down in lightly greased muffin tins or sheet pans.

14. Proof 30 minutes or until almost double in size.

15. Bake at 375° F (190° C) about 25 to 30 minutes or until golden brown. Drizzle glaze over warm rolls.

Glaze

9 oz	Confectioners' sugar	260 g
1½ oz	Skim milk	40 g
1 oz	Vanilla	28 g

Mix all ingredients until smooth.

CROWN ROLLS IN A RING

YIELD: **2 rings**
PORTIONS: **36**
PORTION SIZE: **2 oz (57 g) roll**

Nutritional Information per Serving		
	Amount	*Calories*
Calories		165
Fat	2 g	18
Saturated fatty acid	<1 g	4
Cholesterol	12 mg	
Carbohydrate	31 g	
Added sugars	4 g	
Fiber	1 g	
Protein	5 g	
Sodium	179 mg	
Potassium	80 mg	
Vitamin A	29 RE	
Vitamin C	0 mg	
Calcium	26 mg	
Iron	2 mg	

1 lb	1 oz	Skim milk, scalded and then cooled	490 g
	8 oz	Water	240 g
	2 oz	Margarine, melted	60 g
	½ oz	Salt	10 g
	1¾ oz	Sugar	50 g
	3½ oz	Eggs	100 g
	1 oz	Yeast, dry	28 g
2 lb	12 oz	Bread flour	1250 g
	2 oz	Margarine, melted	60 g
	3½ oz	Sugar	100 g
	⅛ oz	Cinnamon	4 g
5 lb		Total weight	2392 g

PROCEDURE

1. Mix scalded milk with water, sugar, salt, margarine, and eggs.
2. Add dry yeast and one-half the flour. Mix until smooth.
3. Continuing mixing, and add enough remaining flour to make a soft dough.
4. Mix dough at second speed for four minutes.
5. Ferment dough 1½ hours at 80° F (27° C) or until doubled.
6. Scale into two 2½ lb (1077 g) pieces.
7. Divide each piece into eighteen 2 oz (57 g) portions; shape into balls.
8. Lightly brush each ball with melted margarine and roll in cinnamon-sugar mixture.
9. Place balls in single layer in bottom of two lightly greased 10 in (25 cm) tube pans.
10. Proof 30 minutes or until almost doubled.
11. Bake at 375° F (190° C) about 35 to 40 minutes or until golden brown.
12. Remove from pan; turn upright.
13. Garnish with whole maraschino cherries if desired.

PECAN ROLLS

YIELD: 8½ dozen
PORTIONS: 102
PORTION SIZE: 2½ oz (72 g) roll

Nutritional Information per Serving		
	Amount	*Calories*
Calories		225
Fat	7 g	63
Saturated fatty acid	1 g	9
Cholesterol	19 mg	
Carbohydrate	36 g	
Added sugars	17 g	
Fiber	2 g	
Protein	5 g	
Sodium	198 mg	
Potassium	108 mg	
Vitamin A	56 RE	
Vitamin C	<1 mg	
Calcium	31 mg	
Iron	2 mg	

2 lb	12 oz	Water, warm 105° F (41° C)	1250 g
	3 oz	Yeast, dry	85 g
	3 oz	Sugar	85 g
1 lb		Bread flour	450 g
	12 oz	Whole wheat flour	340 g
	8 oz	Sugar	230 g
	8 oz	Margarine, unsalted, room temperature	230 g
	4 oz	Nonfat milk solids	110 g
	1½ oz	Salt	43 g
1 lb		Eggs	450 g
	2 oz	Vanilla	55 g
4 lb	4 oz	Bread flour	1920 g
11 lb	10 oz	Total weight	5248 g

PROCEDURE

1. Add yeast to warm water; let stand 5 minutes.

2. Mix in 3 oz sugar, 1 lb (450 g) bread flour, and whole wheat flour.

3. Ferment 30 minutes. Stir down.

4. Add remaining ingredients, mixing on second speed for 7 to 8 minutes.

5. Ferment dough about 1 hour at 80° F (27° C) or until doubled.

6. Punch down dough.

7. Roll out dough into a rectangle.

8. Brush lightly with egg wash and sprinkle with cinnamon-sugar.

9. Roll up dough, jelly-roll style. Seal edge.

10. Cut into 102 rolls, 1¾ oz (50 g) each. Place in prepared muffin tins.

11. Proof until double in size.

12. Bake at 375° F (190° C) for 15 to 18 minutes or until golden brown.

13. Invert rolls immediately onto parchment-lined sheet pans.

Egg Wash

2 oz	Eggs	55 g
3 oz	Water	85 g

Beat together.

Cinnamon-Sugar

12 oz	Sugar	340 g
½ oz	Cinnamon	14 g

Combine.

Pecan Smear

2 lb		Corn Syrup	900 g
	6 oz	Margarine, unsalted	170 g
	6 oz	Brown sugar	170 g
1 lb	2 oz	Pecans, chopped	500 g
3 lb	14 oz	Total weight	1740 g

1. Bring all ingredients except pecans to a rolling boil. Remove from heat.

2. Grease 102 large muffin tins.

3. Pour ½ oz (1 tbsp) smear into each cup.

4. Place one tablespoon pecans over smear.

ITALIAN PIZZA STICKS

YIELD:	5 dozen
PORTIONS:	60
PORTION SIZE:	1 oz (28 g)

Nutritional Information per Serving

	Amount	Calories
Calories		115
Fat	3 g	27
Saturated fatty acid	1 g	9
Cholesterol	2 mg	
Carbohydrate	17 g	
Added sugars	0 g	
Fiber	1 g	
Protein	4 g	
Sodium	172 mg	
Potassium	114 mg	
Vitamin A	29 RE	
Vitamin C	2 mg	
Calcium	38 mg	
Iron	1 mg	

Note: Nutritional information includes pizza sauce.

Sticks

2 lb		Water, warm, 105° F (41° C)	950 g
	2 oz	Yeast, dry	60 g
2 lb	8 oz	Bread flour	1120 g
	3¾ oz	Olive oil	110 g
	2 tsp	Salt	6 g
	8 oz	Mozzarella cheese, shredded (part skim milk)	230 g
	½ oz	Italian seasoning	15 g
5 lb	6 oz	Total weight	2491 g

PROCEDURE

1. In large bowl, add yeast to warm water and stir to dissolve.
2. Combine remaining ingredients, except the pizza sauce, and add to yeast mixture.
3. Develop dough for 6 minutes on second speed of mixer.
4. Divide dough into five 1 lb (454 g) portions.
5. Divide each portion into 12 pieces.
6. Roll each piece as for a bread stick.
7. Repeat with remaining dough.
8. Bake at 400° F (200° C) for 7 to 10 minutes or until golden brown.

SERVING

1. Warm pizza sauce.
2. Serve with breadsticks for dipping—½ oz (14 g) per stick.

Sauce for Dipping

2 lb 3 oz	Pizza sauce, prepared	1000 g

90-MINUTE FRUIT KUCHEN

YIELD:	3 cakes, 2 lb (900 g) each
PORTIONS:	36
PORTION SIZE:	2¾ oz (80 g)

Nutritional Information per Serving		
	Amount	*Calories*
Calories		190
Fat	4 g	36
Saturated fatty acid	1 g	9
Cholesterol	0 mg	
Carbohydrate	35 mg	
Added sugars	7 g	
Fiber	1 g	
Protein	4 g	
Sodium	53 mg	
Potassium	80 mg	
Vitamin A	37 RE	
Vitamin C	<1 mg	
Calcium	19 mg	
Iron	1 mg	

1 lb	13 oz	Bread flour	830 g
	5 oz	Sugar	130 g
	½ oz	Yeast, dry	14 g
	2 oz	Margarine, softened	70 g
	4 oz	Skim milk, heated to 120°	120 g
	6 oz	Egg whites	170 g
2 lb	10 oz	Fruit pie filling	1190 g
5 lb	8 oz	Total weight of cakes	2524 g

PROCEDURE

1. In small bowl, mix crumb topping ingredients together; set aside.

2. Combine 1 lb (450 g) flour, sugar, and undissolved yeast.

3. Add margarine and hot milk; beat 2 minutes on second speed of the mixer, scraping bowl occasionally.

4. Add egg whites and remaining flour, mixing well.

5. Beat on medium speed 4 minutes until a soft dough forms.

6. Spread dough evenly into three greased 10 in (25 cm) round pans.

7. Spoon one-third of the fruit filling over each ring, leaving the center unfilled. Sprinkle with crumb mixture.

8. Proof about 1 hour at 80° F (27° C).

9. Bake at 375° F (190° C) for 20 to 25 minutes or until golden brown.

10. Drizzle glaze over cakes when cool.

Crumb Topping

3 oz	Bread flour	70 g
2 oz	Margarine, softened	110 g
2 oz	Walnuts	60 g
¼ oz	Cinnamon	7 g

Glaze

3½ oz	Confectiners' sugar	100 g
½ oz	Margarine, hard	14 g
4 oz	Water	110 g

Mix all ingredients. Beat until smooth.

8   QUICK BREADS AND MUFFINS

Muffins have became a breakfast staple that many of us enjoy with our morning beverage. They are also eaten by many on the run who have no time for a sit-down breakfast. Unfortunately, most muffins, especially the gourmet type, are a nutritionally poor way to start the day. Almost all are high in fat and calories—more like cake than muffins.

The recipes that follow will get you off to a good start because they not only are much lower in fat, especially saturated fat, but they add desired fiber to the diet as well.

FORMULAS

Whole-Wheat Waffles	Cranberry Bread and Muffins
Grandmother's Hotcakes	Raisin Bran Muffins
Scones	Cran-Apple Muffins
Buttermilk Biscuits	Pumpkin Muffins
Norwegian Oat Biscuits	Branana Muffins
Apple Coffee Cake	Lemon-Poppyseed Muffins
Soda Bread	Pineapple-Carrot Muffins
Strawberry-Nutmeg Bread	Double Bran Muffins
Banana Bread	Blueberry Muffins
Date-Nut Bread	Apple-Spice Muffins

WHOLE-WHEAT WAFFLES

YIELD: 3 lb 6 oz (1530 g)
PORTIONS: 18
PORTION SIZE: 3 oz (85 g)—1 waffle

	Nutritional Information per Serving	
	Amount	*Calories*
Calories		193
Fat	7 g	63
Saturated fatty acid	1 g	9
Cholesterol	61 mg	
Carbohydrate	22 g	
Added sugars	3 g	
Fiber	1 g	
Protein	12 g	
Sodium	46 mg	
Potassium	154 mg	
Vitamin A	40 RE	
Vitamin C	<1 mg	
Calcium	58 g	
Iron	1 g	

	½ oz	Yeast, dry	14 g
	2 oz	Sugar	60 g
1 lb		Water, warm, 105° F (41° C)	450 g
	10 oz	Pastry flour	280 g
	8½ oz	Whole wheat flour	240 g
	2 oz	Nonfat dry milk	60 g
	3 oz	Oil	85 g
	7 oz	Egg	200 g
	5 oz	Egg white	140 g
3 lb	6 oz	Total weight	1529 g

PROCEDURE

1. Combine yeast, sugar and water. Let stand 5 minutes.
2. Add flours, dry milk, oil, egg, and egg white. Beat on second speed of mixer until blended.
3. Cover and chill 8 hours.
4. Pour 6 oz (170 g) batter (enough for two waffles) onto a lightly greased preheated waffle iron.
5. Cook the waffles until done (waffles should be crisp and golden brown).

GRANDMOTHER'S HOTCAKES

YIELD:	1 full sheet pan, 18 x 26 in (46 x 66 cm), or 34 4 in (10 cm) cakes
PORTIONS:	34
PORTION SIZE:	2 oz (57 g)

Nutritional Information per Serving		
	Amount	*Calories*
Calories		171
Fat	3 g	27
Saturated fatty acid	1 g	9
Cholesterol	65 mg	
Carbohydrate	28 g	
Added sugars	6 g	
Fiber	1 g	
Protein	7 g	
Sodium	317 mg	
Potassium	134 mg	
Vitamin A	24 RE	
Vitamin C	<1 mg	
Calcium	91 mg	
Iron	1 mg	

	10 oz	Pastry flour	285 g
	½ oz	Baking soda	14 g
	1½ tsp	Baking powder	3 g
	4 oz	Sugar	113 g
	2½ oz	Cornmeal	70 g
	3 oz	Oats, quick or regular	85 g
	7 oz	Eggs	200 g
2 lb	3 oz	Buttermilk, lowfat	1000 g
	10 oz	Sour cream, extra light (2 g fat per oz)	285 g
4 lb	8 oz	Total weight	2055 g

PROCEDURE

1. Combine flour, soda, baking powder, and sugar.

2. Stir in cornmeal and oatmeal.

3. Combine eggs, buttermilk, and sour cream.

4. Add to dry mixture, blending just until mixed.

5. Using a 2 oz (57 g) ladle, portion batter onto a lightly greased griddle.

ALTERNATIVE COOKING METHOD:

6. Spread batter in a lightly greased sheet pan, 18 × 26 in (46 × 66 cm).

7. Bake at 400° F (200° C) about 12 minutes; test for doneness as you would a cake. (Watch carefully, as the sugar makes the pancakes brown quickly.)

SCONES

YIELD:	4 dozen
PORTIONS:	48
PORTION SIZE:	2 oz (57 g)

Nutritional Information per Serving		
	Amount	Calories
Calories		163
Fat	5 g	45
Saturated fatty acid	1 g	9
Cholesterol	15 mg	
Carbohydrate	27 g	
Added sugars	4 g	
Fiber	2 g	
Protein	4 g	
Sodium	235 mg	
Potassium	145 mg	
Vitamin A	55 RE	
Vitamin C	<1 mg	
Calcium	40 mg	
Iron	1 mg	

1 lb	8 oz	Pastry flour	680 g
1 lb		Whole wheat pastry flour	450 g
	6 oz	Sugar	170 g
	¾ oz	Baking powder	21 g
	¾ oz	Baking soda	21 g
	¾ tsp	Nutmeg	2 g
	12 oz	Currants	340 g
	8 oz	Margarine	230 g
	6 oz	Eggs	170 g
1 lb	8 oz	Buttermilk	680 g
6 lb	1 oz	Total weight	2764 g

PROCEDURE

1. Combine dry ingredients. Cut in margarine.
2. Beat together eggs and buttermilk. Stir into flour mixture just to moisten.
3. Knead 10 times on a floured surface.
4. Scale dough into six 1 lb (450 g) pieces.
5. Roll each piece to a 9 in (22.5 cm) circle.
6. Place into lightly greased 9 in (22.5 cm) cake pans.
7. Brush with egg wash. Score dough halfway through into eight cuts per pan.
8. Bake at 400° F (200° C) for 15 to 18 minutes or until golden brown.
9. Glaze while warm.

Glaze

| 6 oz | Confectioners' sugar | 170 g |
| 2 oz | Orange juice | 55 g |

Beat until smooth.

Egg Wash

| 2 oz | Eggs | 55 g |
| 3 oz | Water | 85 g |

Beat together.

BUTTERMILK BISCUITS

YIELD: **3 dozen**
PORTIONS: **36 servings**
PORTION SIZE: **2 oz (57 g)**

Nutritional Information per Serving		
	Amount	Calories
Calories		164
Fat	4 g	36
Saturated fatty acid	1 g	9
Cholesterol	<1 mg	
Carbohydrate	27 g	
Added sugars	0 g	
Fiber	1 g	
Protein	4 g	
Sodium	239 mg	
Potassium	68 mg	
Vitamin A	48 RE	
Vitamin C	<1 mg	
Calcium	52 mg	
Iron	2 mg	

2 lb	10 oz	Pastry flour	1200 g
	¾ tsp	Salt	4 g
	1½ oz	Baking powder	42 g
	6 oz	Margarine	170 g
1 lb	8 oz	Buttermilk	680 g
4 lb	10 oz	Total weight	2096 g

PROCEDURE

1. Combine flour, salt, and baking powder. Cut in margarine.
2. Stir in buttermilk only to moisten.
3. Knead 10 times on a floured surface.
4. Roll dough to ½ inch thickness.
5. Cut out 2 oz (57 g) biscuits.
6. Place biscuits on parchment-lined sheet pans.
8. Brush with egg wash.
9. Bake at 425° F (215° C) for 12 to 15 minutes or until golden.

Egg Wash

2 oz	Eggs	55 g
3 oz	Water	85 g

Beat together.

NORWEGIAN OAT BISCUITS

YIELD:	3 dozen
PORTIONS:	36
PORTION SIZE:	2 oz (57 g)

	Nutritional Information per Serving	
	Amount	*Calories*
Calories		168
Fat	5 g	45
Saturated fatty acid	1 g	9
Cholesterol	16 mg	
Carbohydrate	27 g	
Added sugars	8 g	
Fiber	1 g	
Protein	5 g	
Sodium	168 mg	
Potassium	96 mg	
Vitamin A	47 RE	
Vitamin C	0 mg	
Calcium	44 mg	
Iron	1 mg	

	5 oz	Margarine, softened	150 g
	10 ½ oz	Sugar	300 g
	4 oz	Yogurt, lowfat, plain	570 g
	3 ½ oz	Eggs	100 g
	1 ½ oz	Egg whites	33 g
	1 oz	Vanilla	28 g
	14 oz	Oats, quick	400 g
1 lb	1 ½ oz	Pastry flour	500 g
	¼ oz	Baking powder	7 g
	¼ oz	Baking soda	7 g
	⅛ oz	Salt	3 g
4 lb	8 oz	Total weight	2098 g

PROCEDURE

1. Combine margarine, sugar, yogurt, eggs, egg whites, and vanilla. Beat together until light and fluffy.

2. Chop oats in a buffalo chopper or food processor until mixture resembles flour. Combine with other dry ingredients.

3. Gradually add dry ingredients to yogurt mixture, mixing just until moistened.

4. Cover; refrigerate at least one hour or overnight.

5. Divide dough into quarters and divide each quarter into 9 pieces.

6. Shape each piece into an 8 in (20 cm) rope, rolling gently between palms of hands and lightly floured surface.

7. Shape into rings; twist once to form a figure eight. Place on parchment-lined sheet pans.

8. Bake at 375° F (190° C) for 10 to 12 minutes.

APPLE COFFEE CAKE

YIELD:	Four 8 in (20 cm) cakes
PORTIONS:	32 (8 servings per cake)
PORTION SIZE:	3.5 oz (100 g)

Nutritional Information per Serving		
	Amount	*Calories*
Calories		211
Fat	6 g	54
Saturated fatty acid	1 g	9
Cholesterol	0 mg	
Carbohydrate	36 g	
Added sugars	14 g	
Fiber	2 g	
Protein	4 g	
Sodium	167 mg	
Potassium	123 mg	
Vitamin A	74 RE	
Vitamin C	4 mg	
Calcium	31 mg	
Iron	1 mg	

2 lb		Apples, fresh, chopped	900 g
	4 oz	Orange juice	110 g
	¼ oz	Cinnamon	7 g
	12 oz	Sugar	340 g
	8 oz	Margarine	230 g
	1 oz	Vanilla	28 g
1 lb		Egg whites	450 g
	4 oz	Skim milk	110 g
	4 oz	Orange juice	110 g
1 lb		Cake flour	450 g
	6 oz	Whole wheat pastry flour	170 g
	¾ oz	Baking powder	21 g
	2 oz	Brown sugar	55 g
6 lb	10 oz	Total weight	2981 g

PROCEDURE

1. Toss apple pieces with orange juice and cinnamon. Set aside.
2. Cream sugar, margarine, vanilla, and part of the egg whites until light and fluffy.
3. Beat in remaining whites.
4. Combine skim milk and orange juice.
5. Combine flours and baking powder.
6. Add flour mixture to creamed mixture alternately with the milk mixture.
7. Lightly grease four 8 × 2 in (20 cm × 5 cm) cake pans.
8. Scale 17 oz (480 g) of batter into each pan.
9. Top each with 9 oz (250 g) of apple mixture. Sprinkle brown sugar evenly over apples.
10. Bake at 350° F (175° C) for 45 to 55 minutes or until done.
11. While still warm, brush with apricot glaze. Cool.
12. Drizzle with icing.

Glaze

3 oz   Apricot glaze   85 g

Heat before using.

Icing

| 2 oz | Confectioners' sugar | 55 g |
| ½ oz | Water | 14 g |

Beat until smooth.

SODA BREAD

YIELD:	6 loaves, 15 oz (425 g) each	
PORTIONS:	36 (6 servings per loaf)	
PORTION SIZE:	2 ½ oz (70 g)	

Nutritional Information per Serving		
	Amount	*Calories*
Calories		166
Fat	3 g	27
Saturated fatty acid	1 g	9
Cholesterol	<1 mg	
Carbohydrate	31 g	
Added sugars	1 g	
Fiber	2 g	
Protein	5 g	
Sodium	161 mg	
Potassium	132 mg	
Vitamin A	26 RE	
Vitamin C	<1 mg	
Calcium	42 mg	
Iron	2 mg	

2 lb		Pastry flour	900 g
1 lb		Whole wheat flour	450 g
	½ oz	Baking soda	14 g
	¼ oz	Cream of tartar	7 g
	1 oz	Sugar	28 g
	4 oz	Margarine	110 g
2 lb	5 oz	Buttermilk	1070 g
5 lb	11 oz	Total weight	2579 g

PROCEDURE

1. Combine flours, baking soda, cream of tartar, and sugar. Cut in margarine.
2. Stir in buttermilk.
3. Knead 10 times on a floured board.
4. Scale into six 15 oz (425 g) pieces.
5. Place on parchment-lined sheet pans and flatten slightly.
6. Cut an X ½ inch deep on tops.
7. Brush lightly with egg wash.
8. Bake at 400° F (200° C) for 35 minutes or until done.

Egg Wash

2 oz	Eggs	55 g
3 oz	Water	85 g

Beat together.

STRAWBERRY-NUTMEG BREAD

YIELD:	2 loaves, 1 lb 12 oz (795 g) each
PORTIONS:	28
PORTION SIZE:	2 oz (57 g)

Nutritional Information per Serving		
	Amount	Calories
Calories		186
Fat	6 g	54
Saturated fatty acid	1 g	9
Cholesterol	15 mg	
Carbohydrate	30 g	
Added sugars	9 g	
Fiber	2 g	
Protein	4 g	
Sodium	124 mg	
Potassium	78 mg	
Vitamin A	11 RE	
Vitamin C	5 mg	
Calcium	10 mg	
Iron	1 mg	

1 lb	2 oz	Pastry flour	510 g
	9 oz	Sugar	255 g
	6 oz	Cornmeal	170 g
	1/4 oz	Nutmeg	7 g
	1/8 oz	Salt	3 g
	1/8 oz	Baking soda	4 g
	2 oz	Walnuts, chopped	60 g
	12 oz	Frozen strawberries, quartered	340 g
	4 oz	Oil	110 g
	3 1/2 oz	Eggs	100 g
	3 1/2 oz	Egg whites	100 g
	2 oz	Apple juice	60 g
3 lb	12 oz	Total weight	1719 g

PROCEDURE

1. Combine dry ingredients, including walnuts.
2. Combine strawberries, oil, eggs, egg whites, and apple juice.
3. Add strawberry mixture to dry ingredients; mix just to moisten dry ingredients.
4. Divide batter between two lightly greased 9 × 5 × 3 in (22.5 × 12.5 × 7.5 cm) loaf pans.
5. Bake at 350° F (175° C) 45 to 60 minutes or until done.

NOTE

To make Strawberry-Nutmeg Muffins, portion 2 oz (57 g) batter into each of 30 paper-lined muffin cups. Bake at 375° F (190° C) 20 to 25 minutes.

BANANA BREAD

YIELD:	5 loaves 1 lb 4 oz (560 g) each
PORTIONS:	40 (8 servings per loaf)
PORTION SIZE:	2 ½ oz (70 g) slice

Nutritional Information per Serving		
	Amount	*Calories*
Calories		185
Fat	4 g	36
Saturated fatty acid	<1 mg	8
Cholesterol	12 mg	
Carbohydrate	34 g	
Added sugars	8 g	
Fiber	2 g	
Protein	4 g	
Sodium	166 mg	
Potassium	174 mg	
Vitamin A	50 RE	
Vitamin C	2 mg	
Calcium	33 mg	
Iron	1 mg	

	12 oz	Sugar	340 g
	6 oz	Margarine	170 g
	½ oz	Vanilla	15 g
	4 oz	Eggs	110 g
	4 oz	Egg whites	110 g
2 lb	4 oz	Bananas, pureed	1000 g
1 lb	4 oz	Pastry flour	560 g
1 lb		Whole wheat flour	450 g
	1½ oz	Baking powder	43 g
	¼ oz	Cinnamon	7 g
6 lb	4 oz	Total weight	2805 g

PROCEDURE

1. Cream sugar, margarine, vanilla, and eggs until light and fluffy.
2. Stir in egg whites and bananas.
3. Combine flours, baking powder, and cinnamon. Stir into banana mixture.
4. Lightly grease five 7⅜ × 3⅝ in (19 × 9 cm) loaf pans.
5. Scale 1 lb 4 oz (560 g) batter into each loaf pan.
6. Bake at 350° F (175° C) for 50 to 55 minutes or until done.

DATE-NUT BREAD

YIELD: 6 loaves, 1 lb 4 oz (560 g) each
PORTIONS: 48 (8 servings per loaf)
PORTION SIZE: 2 ½ oz (70 g)

2 lb		Water, boiling	900 g
1 lb	12 oz	Dates, chopped	800 g
	3 oz	Margarine	85 g
1 lb	8 oz	Pastry flour	680 g
	8 oz	Whole wheat flour	230 g
	12 oz	Sugar	340 g
	¾ oz	Baking soda	21 g
	¾ oz	Baking powder	21 g
	½ oz	Orange peel, grated	14 g
	4 oz	Walnuts, chopped	110 g
	8 oz	Egg whites	230 g
7 lb	9 oz	Total weight	3431 g

PROCEDURE

1. Combine water, dates, and margarine. Let cool 5 minutes.
2. Mix together dry ingredients.
3. Add date mixture to dry ingredients along with egg whites. Stir just to moisten.
4. Lightly grease six 7⅜ × 3⅝ in (19 × 9 cm) loaf pans.
5. Scale 1 lb 4 oz (560 g) batter into each loaf pan.
6. Bake at 350° F (175° C) for 40 to 45 minutes or until done.

Nutritional Information per Serving

	Amount	Calories
Calories		172
Fat	3 g	27
Saturated fatty acid	<1 g	4
Cholesterol	0 mg	
Carbohydrate	34 g	
Added sugars	7 g	
Fiber	2.5 g	
Protein	3 g	
Sodium	196 mg	
Potassium	163 mg	
Vitamin A	19 RE	
Vitamin C	<1 mg	
Calcium	22 mg	
Iron	1 mg	

CRANBERRY BREAD AND MUFFINS

Nutritional Information per Serving (Bread)		
	Amount	*Calories*
Calories		194
Fat	6 g	54
Saturated fatty acid	<1 g	4
Cholesterol	12 mg	
Carbohydrate	32 g	
Added sugars	11 g	
Fiber	2 g	
Protein	5 g	
Sodium	198 mg	
Potassium	121 mg	
Vitamin A	9 RE	
Vitamin C	9 mg	
Calcium	12 mg	
Iron	1 mg	

Nutritional Information per Serving (Muffins)		
	Amount	*Calories*
Calories		162
Fat	5 g	45
Saturated fatty acid	<1 g	3
Cholesterol	10 mg	
Carbohydrate	27 g	
Added sugars	9 g	
Fiber	2 g	
Protein	4 g	
Sodium	169 mg	
Potassium	101 mg	
Vitamin A	7 RE	
Vitamin C	7 mg	
Calcium	10 mg	
Iron	1 mg	

YIELD: 5 loaves 1 lb 4 oz (560 g) each, or 4 dozen muffins
PORTIONS: 40 (8 servings per loaf) servings or 48 muffins
PORTION SIZE: 2 ½ oz (70 g) bread slice or 2 oz (57 g) muffin

1 lb		Cranberries, fresh or frozen	450 g
	½ oz	Orange peel, grated	14 g
1 lb	8 oz	Orange juice	680 g
	4 oz	Eggs	110 g
	4 oz	Egg whites	110 g
	4 oz	Oil	110 g
1 lb	4 oz	Pastry flour	560 g
	12 oz	Whole wheat flour	340 g
1 lb		Sugar	450 g
	1 oz	Baking soda	28 g
	6 oz	Walnuts, chopped	170 g
6 lb	12 oz	Total weight	3022 g

PROCEDURE

1. Coarsely chop cranberries. Stir in orange peel.
2. Beat in orange juice, eggs, egg whites, and oil.
3. Add dry ingredients and mix just to moisten.
4. Scale either for bread or muffins.

SCALING FOR BREADS

1. Lightly grease five 7⅜ × 3⅝ in (19 × 9 cm) loaf pans.
2. Scale (560 g) batter 1 lb 4 oz into each loaf pan.
3. Bake at 350° F (175° C) for 50 to 55 minutes or until done.

SCALING FOR MUFFINS

1. Line 4 dozen muffin cups with paper liners.
2. Portion 2 oz (57 g) batter into each muffin cup.
3. Bake at 400° F (200° C) for 18 to 22 minutes or until done.

RAISIN BRAN MUFFINS

YIELD:	4 dozen muffins
PORTIONS:	48
PORTION SIZE:	2 oz (57 g)

	Nutritional Information per Serving	
	Amount	Calories
Calories		143
Fat	4 g	36
Saturated fatty acid	<1 g	4
Cholesterol	11 mg	
Carbohydrate	27 g	
Added sugars	9 g	
Fiber	2 g	
Protein	4 g	
Sodium	188 mg	
Potassium	167 mg	
Vitamin A	6 RE	
Vitamin C	<1 mg	
Calcium	32 mg	
Iron	2 mg	

5 oz		Oil	140 g
8 oz		Honey	230 g
4 oz		Eggs	110 g
4 oz		Egg whites	110 g
1 lb	10 oz	Buttermilk	730 g
8 oz		Brown sugar	230 g
1 lb	6 oz	Pastry flour	630 g
	10 oz	Wheat bran	280 g
	1 oz	Baking soda	28 g
8 oz		Raisins	230 g
6 lb		Total weight	2718 g

PROCEDURE

1. Mix together oil, honey, eggs, egg whites, and buttermilk.
2. Add dry ingredients, mixing just to moisten. Stir in raisins.
3. Line 4 dozen muffin cups with paper liners.
4. Portion 2 oz (57 g) batter into each muffin cup.
5. Bake at 400° F (200° C) for 18 to 22 minutes or until done.

CRAN-APPLE MUFFINS

YIELD: 4 dozen
PORTIONS: 48
PORTION SIZE: 2 oz (57 g)

Nutritional Information per Serving		
	Amount	*Calories*
Calories		147
Fat	5 g	45
Saturated fatty acid	1 g	9
Cholesterol	0 mg	
Carbohydrate	24 g	
Added sugars	9 g	
Fiber	1 g	
Protein	2 g	
Sodium	51 mg	
Potassium	43 mg	
Vitamin A	4 RE	
Vitamin C	1 mg	
Calcium	14 mg	
Iron	1 mg	

Batter

1 lb	6 oz	Pastry flour	630 g
	12 oz	Sugar	350 g
	¼ oz	Cinnamon	7 g
	¼ oz	Baking soda	7 g
	1 tsp	Baking powder	2 g
	8 oz	Egg whites	230 g
	13½ oz	Apple, shredded	385 g
	10 oz	Skim milk	280 g
	13½ oz	Oil	385 g

Filling

1 lb	1 oz	Cranberry sauce, whole	490 g
	¼ oz	Orange peel, shredded	6 g
6 lb		Total weight	2772 g

PROCEDURE

1. Combine flour, sugar, cinnamon, baking soda, baking powder, and salt.

2. Combine egg whites, apple, milk, and oil.

3. Add egg mixture all at once to dry ingredients. Mix just until moistened.

4. Portion 2 oz (57 g) batter into each of 48 paper muffin cups. Make a well in center of each with back of a spoon.

5. Combine cranberry sauce and orange peel in a small bowl.

6. Spoon 2 teaspoons of cranberry filling into each well.

7. Bake at 375° F (190° C) about 18 to 20 minutes. Glaze while warm.

Glaze

2½ oz	Confectioners' sugar	75 g
1½ oz	Orange juice	40 g

Beat until smooth.

PUMPKIN MUFFINS

YIELD:	4 ½ dozen
PORTIONS:	54 muffins
PORTION SIZE:	2 oz (57 g)

	Nutritional Information per Serving	
	Amount	Calories
Calories		157
Fat	5 g	45
Saturated fatty acid	<1 g	5
Cholesterol	11 mg	
Carbohydrate	27 g	
Added sugars	13 g	
Fiber	1 g	
Protein	3 g	
Sodium	92 mg	
Potassium	60 mg	
Vitamin A	316 RE	
Vitamin C	<1 mg	
Calcium	13 mg	
Iron	1 mg	

	3 oz	Pastry flour	85 g
	3 oz	Sugar	85 g
	½ tsp	Cinnamon	1 g
	2 oz	Margarine	50 g
	5 oz	Eggs	140 g
	5 oz	Egg whites	140 g
	6 oz	Oil	170 g
1 lb	10 oz	Pumpkin, canned	730 g
	8 oz	Buttermilk	230 g
1 lb	6 oz	Sugar	630 g
1 lb	12 oz	Pastry flour	800 g
	¾ oz	Baking soda	21 g
	1 tbsp	Cinnamon	7 g
	1 tsp	Nutmeg	3 g
	½ tsp	Cloves	1 g
	½ tsp	Allspice	1 g
6 lb	13 oz	Total weight	3094 g

PROCEDURE

1. Combine first three ingredients. Cut in margarine. Set aside for streusel topping.

2. Beat together eggs, egg whites, oil, pumpkin, and buttermilk.

3. Stir in sugar, flour, baking soda, and spices just to moisten.

4. Line 4½ dozen muffin cups with paper liners.

5. Portion 2 oz (57 g) batter into each muffin cup.

6. Sprinkle reserved streusel topping evenly over muffins.

7. Bake at 375° F (190° C) for 18 to 22 minutes or until done.

BRANANA MUFFINS

YIELD:	3½ dozen
PORTIONS:	36
PORTION SIZE:	2 oz (57 g)

	4 oz	Oil	120 g
	10½ oz	Egg whites	300 g
1 lb	12 oz	Ripe bananas, pureed	790 g
	6 oz	Sugar	165 g
	1 oz	Vanilla	28 g
	8 oz	Bran cereal flakes, crushed	260 g
	15 oz	Pastry flour	600 g
	¼ oz	Baking soda	6 g
	⅔ oz	Baking powder	19 g
4 lb	8 oz	Total weight	2288 g

Nutritional Information per Serving

	Amount	Calories
Calories		135
Fat	4 g	36
Saturated fatty acid	1 g	9
Cholesterol	0 mg	
Carbohydrate	24 g	
Added sugars	5 g	
Fiber	2 g	
Protein	3 g	
Sodium	162 mg	
Potassium	150 mg	
Vitamin A	66 RE	
Vitamin C	2 mg	
Calcium	18 mg	
Iron	4 mg	

PROCEDURE

1. Combine oil, egg whites, bananas, sugar, and vanilla. Mix thoroughly.

2. Add dry ingredients; mix just until moistened.

3. Portion 2 oz (57 g) batter into prepared muffin cups (either use paper liners or grease lightly).

4. Bake at 400° F (200° C) about 20 minutes or until done.

LEMON-POPPYSEED MUFFINS

YIELD: 3½ dozen
PORTIONS: 42
PORTION SIZE: 2 oz (57 g)

	Nutritional Information per Serving		
		Amount	*Calories*
Calories			148
Fat		4 g	36
Saturated fatty acid		2 g	18
Cholesterol		5 mg	
Carbohydrate		24 g	
Added sugars		10 g	
Fiber		<1 g	
Protein		4 g	
Sodium		218 mg	
Potassium		60 mg	
Vitamin A		45 RE	
Vitamin C		2 mg	
Calcium		50 mg	
Iron		9 mg	

	5 oz	Margarine, softened	140 g	
	10 oz	Sugar	285 g	
	9 oz	Egg whites	255 g	
		Extra light sour cream		
1 lb	4 oz	(2 g fat per oz)	570 g	
	¾ oz	Baking soda	19 g	
	12 oz	Skim milk	340 g	
1 lb	8 oz	Pastry flour	685 g	
		Grated rind of 2 lemons		
	2 oz	Poppyseeds	60 g	
5 lb	3 oz	Total weight	2354 g	

PROCEDURE

1. Cream margarine and sugar. Add egg whites and beat until fluffy.

2. Add baking soda to sour cream. Blend into sugar mixture.

3. Add milk alternately with flour and stir lightly.

4. Fold in lemon rind and poppyseeds.

5. Portion 2 oz (57 g) batter into each of 42 prepared muffin tins (either use paper liners or grease lightly).

6. Bake at 400° F (200° C) about 25 minutes or until light brown. Glaze while warm.

Glaze

5 oz   Lemon juice, fresh   140 g
4 oz   Sugar   110 g

Dissolve sugar in lemon juice and mix thoroughly.

PINEAPPLE-CARROT MUFFINS

YIELD: 3 dozen muffins
PORTIONS: 36
PORTION SIZE: 2 oz (57 g)

Nutritional Information per Serving		
	Amount	*Calories*
Calories		115
Fat	3	27
Saturated fatty acid	<1 g	3
Cholesterol	<1 mg	
Carbohydrate	20 g	
Added sugars	6 g	
Fiber	2 g	
Protein	3 g	
Sodium	101 mg	
Potassium	129 mg	
Vitamin A	178 RE	
Vitamin C	2 mg	
Calcium	43 mg	
Iron	1 mg	

1 lb		Yogurt, nonfat, plain	450 g
	8 oz	Brown sugar	230 g
	4 oz	Oil	110 g
	4 oz	Egg whites	110 g
1 lb		Pineapple, crushed canned, undrained	450 g
	6 oz	Carrots, finely grated	170 g
	12 oz	Pastry flour	340 g
	6 oz	Wheat bran	170 g
	¾ oz	Baking powder	21 g
	¼ oz	Baking soda	7 g
4 lb	9 oz	Total weight	2058 g

PROCEDURE

1. Beat together yogurt, brown sugar, oil, and egg whites.
2. Stir in pineapple and grated carrots.
3. Stir in dry ingredients just to moisten.
4. Line 36 muffin cups with paper liners.
5. Portion with 2 oz (57 g) batter into each muffin cup.
6. Bake at 400° F (200° C) for 18 to 22 minutes or until done.

DOUBLE BRAN MUFFINS

YIELD: 4½ dozen
PORTIONS: 54
PORTION SIZE: 2 oz (57 g)

	16 oz	Water, boiling	450 g
	3¾ oz	Wheat bran	100 g
	9 oz	Oat bran	252 g
2 lb	2 oz	Buttermilk	980 g
	7 oz	Eggs	200 g
	3¾ oz	Oil	100 g
	½ oz	Baking soda	15 g
	14 oz	Sugar	400 g
	7¾ oz	Pastry flour	220 g
	12½ oz	Whole wheat flour	360 g
6 lb	12 oz	Total weight	3077 g

PROCEDURE

1. Mix wheat bran and boiling water. Allow to cool.

2. Add oat bran, buttermilk, eggs and oil. Mix well.

3. Add baking soda, sugar, and flours. Stir together just until mixed.

4. Portion 2 oz (57 g) batter into prepared muffin cups (either use paper liners or grease lightly).

5. Bake at 400° F (200° C) for 20 minutes or until done.

Nutritional Information per Serving		
	Amount	Calories
Calories		123
Fat	3 g	27
Saturated fatty acid	<1 mg	
Cholesterol	19 mg	
Carbohydrate	22 g	
Added sugars	7 g	
Fiber	3 g	
Protein	3 g	
Sodium	88 mg	
Potassium	124 mg	
Vitamin A	6 RE	
Vitamin C	<1 mg	
Calcium	29 mg	
Iron	1 mg	

BLUEBERRY MUFFINS

YIELD:	4½ dozen muffins
PORTIONS:	54 muffins
PORTION SIZE:	2 oz (57 g)

Nutritional Information per Serving		
	Amount	*Calories*
Calories		146
Fat	5 g	45
Saturated fatty acid	<1 g	4
Cholesterol	<1 mg	
Carbohydrate	23 g	
Added sugars	10 g	
Fiber	2 g	
Protein	4 g	
Sodium	160 mg	
Potassium	95 mg	
Vitamin A	11 RE	
Vitamin C	<1 mg	
Calcium	53 mg	
Iron	1 mg	

	8 oz	Oil	230 g
	8 oz	Egg whites	230 g
2 lb		Skim milk	900 g
1 lb	4 oz	Pastry flour	560 g
1 lb	4 oz	Whole wheat pastry flour	560 g
	10 oz	Sugar	280 g
	2½ oz	Baking powder	70 g
	1 tsp	Cinnamon	2 g
1 lb		Blueberries, fresh or frozen	450 g
7 lb	4 oz	Total weight	3282 g

PROCEDURE

1. Mix together oil, egg whites, and skim milk.

2. Stir in dry ingredients just to moisten.

3. Carefully fold in blueberries.

4. Line 4½ dozen muffin cups with paper liners.

5. Portion 2 oz (57 g) batter into each muffin cup.

6. Bake at 400° F (200° C) for 18 to 22 minutes or until done.

APPLE-SPICE MUFFINS

YIELD:	4 dozen
PORTIONS:	48
PORTION SIZE:	2 oz (57 g)

Nutritional Information per Serving		
	Amount	*Calories*
Calories		121
Fat	4 g	36
Saturated fatty acid	<1 g	3
Cholesterol	<1 mg	
Carbohydrate	19 g	
Added sugars	5 g	
Fiber	1 g	
Protein	3 g	
Sodium	180 mg	
Potassium	94 mg	
Vitamin A	2 RE	
Vitamin C	<1 mg	
Calcium	35 mg	
Iron	1 mg	

	6 oz	Egg whites	170 g
	6 oz	Oil	170 g
1 lb	14 oz	Buttermilk	850 g
1 lb		Pastry flour	450 g
	10 oz	Whole wheat flour	280 g
	6 oz	Brown sugar	170 g
	½ oz	Baking powder	14 g
	¾ oz	Baking soda	21 g
	¼ oz	Cinnamon	7 g
	¼ tsp	Nutmeg	2 g
1 lb	6 oz	Apples, canned, water-packed, drained and finely chopped	620 g
6 lb	1 oz	Total weight	2754 g

PROCEDURE

1. Beat together egg whites, oil, and buttermilk.

2. Add dry ingredients, stirring just to moisten.

3. Carefully stir in apples.

4. Lightly grease 48 muffin cups.

5. Portion 2 oz (57 g) batter into each muffin cup. Do not use paper liners, or muffins may stick.

6. Sprinkle tops of each muffin with ½ teaspoon cinnamon-sugar.

7. Bake at 400° F (200° C) for 18 to 22 minutes or until done.

Cinnamon-Sugar

2 oz	Sugar	55 g
1 tsp	Cinnamon	4 g

Combine sugar and cinnamon.

9

COOKIES AND BARS

Even though they are a favorite snack of kids and grown-ups alike, most cookies and bars are on the nutritional no-no list because of their high fat and calorie contents. The solution is not to forbid these goodies—it probably won't work anyway—but to make them healthier so they become part of a moderate diet.

The sugar and fat amounts have been reduced in these formulas without sacrificing any of the characteristics we expect from these products. Cookies and bars are some of the easiest formulas to change nutritionally, so try the substitutions and modifications mentioned earlier on your favorite formulas to make them more healthful.

FORMULAS

Jam-Filled Cookies

Meringue Kisses

Icebox Cookies

Gingersnaps

Hermits

Creative Cutout Cookies

Choc-Oat Chip Cookies

Oatmeal-Raisin Cookies

Orange-Molasses Drop
   Cookies

Strawberry Bars

Sour Cream Brownies

Cheesecake Bars

Marble Cheesecake Bars

Pumpkin Bars

Raspberry-Fudge Bars

Apple Bars

Fruit Bars

Date Bars

JAM-FILLED COOKIES

YIELD: 7 dozen
PORTIONS: 84
PORTION SIZE: 1 oz (28 g)

Nutritional Information per Serving		
	Amount	*Calories*
Calories		121
Fat	3 g	27
Saturated fatty acid	1 g	9
Cholesterol	<1 mg	
Carbohydrate	21 g	
Added sugars	14 g	
Fiber	1 g	
Protein	2 g	
Sodium	82 mg	
Potassium	45 mg	
Vitamin A	41 RE	
Vitamin C	<1 mg	
Calcium	14 mg	
Iron	1 mg	

1 lb	4 oz	Sugar	560 g
	12 oz	Margarine	340 g
	8 oz	Egg whites	230 g
	1 oz	Vanilla	28 g
1 lb	6 oz	Pastry flour	620 g
1 lb		Whole wheat pastry flour	450 g
	1 oz	Baking powder	28 g
	4 oz	Skim milk	110 g
1 lb	5 oz	Fruit jam, sugar-free (fruit juice–sweetened)	600 g
6 lb	9 oz	Total weight	2966 g

PROCEDURE

1. Cream sugar and margarine until light and fluffy.
2. Add egg whites in stages, beating well after each addition. Stir in vanilla.
3. Combine flours and baking powder. Add to creamed mixture.
4. Cover and chill dough overnight.
5. Roll out dough. Cut with round cookie cutter to yield eighty-four 1 oz (28 g) cookies.
6. Brush edges of cookies with water.
7. Pipe ¼ oz (7 g) — ½ tbsp — jam onto cookies.
8. Fold each cookie in half and press edges together to seal.
9. Place on parchment-lined sheet pans.
10. Bake at 375° F (190° C) for 10 to 12 minutes or until golden around edges.

MERINGUE KISSES

YIELD: 4 dozen
PORTIONS: 48
PORTION SIZE: ½ oz (14 g)

8 oz	Egg whites	230 g
11 oz	Sugar	310 g
2 oz	Crisp rice cereal	55 g
3 oz	Raisins	85 g
1 lb 8 oz	Total weight	680 g

Nutritional Information per Serving		
	Amount	*Calories*
Calories		37
Fat	0 g	0
Saturated fatty acid	0 g	0
Cholesterol	0 mg	
Carbohydrate	9 g	
Added sugars	7 g	
Fiber	<1 g	
Protein	1 g	
Sodium	15 mg	
Potassium	28 mg	
Vitamin A	<1 RE	
Vitamin C	<1 mg	
Calcium	5 mg	
Iron	<1 mg	

PROCEDURE

1. Whip egg whites to soft peaks.

2. Gradually add sugar and whip to a firm meringue.

3. Stir in cereal and raisins.

4. Bag out ½ oz (14 g) batter per cookie onto parchment-lined sheet pans, or portion with a scoop that gives the desired weight.

5. Bake at 250° F (125° C) for 45 to 55 minutes or until crisp.

ICEBOX COOKIES

YIELD: 4 dozen
PORTIONS: 48
PORTION SIZE: 1 oz (28 g)

	Nutritional Information per Serving	
	Amount	*Calories*
Calories		106
Fat	4 g	36
Saturated fatty acid	1 g	9
Cholesterol	0 mg	
Carbohydrate	16 g	
Added sugars	7 g	
Fiber	1 g	
Protein	2 g	
Sodium	60 mg	
Potassium	36 mg	
Vitamin A	47 RE	
Vitamin C	<1 mg	
Calcium	6 mg	
Iron	1 mg	

8 oz	Margarine	230 g
12 oz	Sugar	340 g
½ oz	Vanilla	14 g
8 oz	Egg whites	230 g
12 oz	Pastry flour	340 g
8 oz	Whole wheat pastry flour	230 g
1 tsp	Baking powder	5 g
3 lb	Total weight	1389 g

PROCEDURE

1. Cream margarine, sugar, and vanilla until light and fluffy.
2. Beat in egg whites gradually.
3. Combine flours and baking powder. Add to creamed mixture.
4. Shape dough into a log, and chill overnight.
5. Slice log into 48 1 oz (28 g) cookies.
6. Place cookies onto parchment-lined sheet pans.
7. Bake at 375° F (190° C) for 7 to 10 minutes, or until golden brown around edges.

GINGERSNAPS

YIELD:	6 ⅓ dozen
PORTIONS:	76
PORTION SIZE:	1 oz (28 g)

	8 oz	Margarine	230 g
	8 oz	Sugar	230 g
	¼ oz	Ginger	7 g
1 lb	4 oz	Molasses	550 g
	½ oz	Baking soda	14 g
	8 oz	Water	230 g
1 lb	4 oz	Pastry flour	560 g
	12 oz	Whole wheat pastry flour	340 g
4 lb	12 oz	Total weight	2161 g

Nutritional Information per Serving		
	Amount	*Calories*
Calories		92
Fat	3 g	27
Saturated fatty acid	<1 g	4
Cholesterol	0 mg	
Carbohydrate	16 g	
Added sugars	10 g	
Fiber	1 g	
Protein	1 g	
Sodium	81 mg	
Potassium	98 mg	
Vitamin A	30 RE	
Vitamin C	<1 mg	
Calcium	16 mg	
Iron	1 mg	

PROCEDURE

1. Cream margarine, sugar, and ginger until light and fluffy.

2. Beat in molasses, baking soda, and water.

3. Add flours.

4. Portion out 76 1 oz (28 g) cookies onto parchment-lined sheet pans.

5. Flatten cookies slightly.

6. Bake at 375° F (190° C) for 10 to 12 minutes or until done.

HERMITS

YIELD:	7 dozen
PORTIONS:	84
PORTION SIZE:	1 oz (28 g)

Nutritional Information per Serving		
	Amount	Calories
Calories		93
Fat	2 g	18
Saturated fatty acid	<1 g	4
Cholesterol	0 mg	
Carbohydrate	17 g	
Added sugars	5 g	
Fiber	1 g	
Protein	2 g	
Sodium	98 mg	
Potassium	78 mg	
Vitamin A	27 RE	
Vitamin C	<1 mg	
Calcium	11 mg	
Iron	1 mg	

	12 oz	Sugar	340 g
	7 oz	Molasses	200 g
	8 oz	Margarine	230 g
	¾ oz	Baking soda	21 g
	1 tsp	Cinnamon	2 g
	4 oz	Egg whites	110 g
1 lb	2 oz	Pastry flour	500 g
1 lb	2 oz	Whole wheat pastry flour	500 g
	6 oz	Water	170 g
	8 oz	Raisins	230 g
	2 oz	Skim milk	55 g
5 lb	4 oz	Total weight	2358 g

PROCEDURES

1. Cream sugar, molasses, margarine, baking soda, and cinnamon until light and fluffy.
2. Beat in egg whites.
3. Add flours, water, and raisins.
4. Scale dough into seven 12 oz (340 g) pieces.
5. Line two 18 × 26 in (46 × 66 cm) sheet pans with parchment paper.
6. Roll each piece into a log to fit lengthwise onto the sheet pan.
7. Place four rolls lengthwise on one sheet pan and three rolls on the other.
8. Flatten each log slightly, and then brush lightly with skim milk.
9. Bake at 350° F (175° C) for 12 to 15 minutes or until edges are light brown but middles are still soft; do not overbake. Cool.
10. Cut each strip into 12 bars.

CREATIVE CUTOUT COOKIES

YIELD:	4 dozen
PORTIONS:	48
PORTION SIZE:	1 oz (28 g)

	Nutritional Information per Serving		
		Amount	*Calories*
Calories			114
Fat		4 g	36
	Saturated fatty acid	1 g	9
Cholesterol		9 mg	
Carbohydrate		17 g	
	Added sugars	5 g	
Fiber		1 g	
Protein		2 g	
Sodium		107 mg	
Potassium		37 mg	
Vitamin A		64 mg	
Vitamin C		0 mg	
Calcium		8 mg	
Iron		1 mg	

	7 oz	Confectioners' sugar	200 g
	10 oz	Margarine, soft-spread, low-fat	300 g
	3⅕ oz	Eggs	100 g
	2 oz	Egg whites	70 g
	½ oz	Vanilla	14 g
	¼ oz	Almond extract	7 g
	2 oz	Skim milk	70 g
	7 oz	Oats, quick	200 g
1 lb	3 oz	Pastry flour	560 g
	¼ oz	Baking soda	7 g
3 lb		Total weight	1530 g

PROCEDURE

1. Cream together confectioners' sugar, margarine, eggs, egg whites, flavorings, and milk.

2. Chop oats in a chopper or food processor until mixture resembles flour. Combine oat flour with other dry ingredients.

3. Stir the dry ingredients into the creamed mixture.

4. Remove dough from bowl, wrap, and refrigerate two hours or until firm.

5. Roll out cold dough to ¼ in thickness. Cut into desired shapes with cookie cutters.

6. Place cookies onto parchment-lined sheet pans.

7. Lightly brush each cookie with egg wash; sprinkle with ¼ tsp colored sugar.

8. Bake at 375° F (190° C) for 7 to 8 minutes or until lightly browned. (These cookies are better if served the day after baking.)

Decoration

1¾ oz	Colored sanding sugar	50 g

Egg Wash

2 oz	Egg whites	70 g
2 tbsp	Water	28 g

Beat egg whites and water together to form egg wash.

CHOC-OAT CHIP COOKIES

YIELD:	8 dozen
PORTIONS:	84
PORTION SIZE:	1 oz (28 g)

	12 oz	Margarine, soft-spread, low-fat	340 g
	7 oz	Eggs	200 g
	10½ oz	Sugar	300 g
	11½ oz	Brown sugar	330 g
	3 oz	Skim milk	85 g
	14 oz	Oats	400 g
1 lb	1½ oz	Pastry flour	500 g
	¼ oz	Baking soda	7 g
	1 tsp	Baking powder	4 g
	8 oz	Chocolate chips, semisweet	230 g
5 lb	4 oz	Total weight	2400 g

Nutritional Information per Serving

	Amount	Calories
Calories		107
Fat	4 g	36
Saturated fatty acid	1 g	9
Cholesterol	13 mg	
Carbohydrate	16 g	
Added sugars	7 g	
Fiber	0.5 g	
Protein	2 g	
Sodium	87 mg	
Potassium	51 mg	
Vitamin A	45 RE	
Vitamin C	0 mg	
Calcium	12 mg	
Iron	1 g	

PROCEDURE

1. Cream margarine and eggs. Add sugars and milk and mix well.

2. Chop oats in a chopper or food processor until mixture resembles flour. Mix oat flour, pastry flour, baking soda, and baking powder together. Add to creamed mixture and mix well.

3. Fold in chocolate chips.

4. Portion out 84 1 oz (28 g) cookies onto parchment-lined sheet pans.

5. Bake at 350° F (175° C) for 10 to 12 minutes or until done. Remove to wire racks and cool.

OATMEAL-RAISIN COOKIES

YIELD:	6 ½ dozen
PORTIONS:	78 cookies
PORTION SIZE:	1 oz (28 g)

	Nutritional Information per Serving	
	Amount	*Calories*
Calories		108
Fat	4 g	36
Saturated fatty acid	<1 g	6
Cholesterol	5 mg	
Carbohydrate	18 g	
Added sugars	7 g	
Fiber	1 g	
Protein	2 g	
Sodium	101 g	
Potassium	77 g	
Vitamin A	40 RE	
Vitamin C	<1 mg	
Calcium	12 mg	
Iron	1 mg	

10 ½ oz	Margarine, softened	300 g
9 ½ oz	Sugar	270 g
10 oz	Brown sugar	290 g
3 ½ oz	Eggs	100 g
3 ½ oz	Egg whites	100 g
½ oz	Vanilla	14 g
2 oz	Water	60 g
9 oz	White pastry flour	255 g
9 oz	Whole wheat flour	255 g
12 oz	Oats, regular or quick	340 g
¼ oz	Baking soda	7 g
¼ oz	Salt	7 g
¼ oz	Cinnamon	7 g
¼ oz	Nutmeg	7 g
10 oz	Raisins, dark seedless	285 g
5 lb	Total weight	2300 g

PROCEDURE

1. Cream margarine, sugars, eggs, egg whites, vanilla, and water together.

2. Mix dry ingredients together; blend into creamed mixture (if using a mixer, set at at low speed).

3. Fold in raisins.

4. Portion 78 1 oz (28 g) cookies onto parchment-lined sheet pans.

5. Bake at 350° F (175° C) for 15 to 18 minutes or until done. Remove to wire racks and cool.

ORANGE-MOLASSES DROP COOKIES

YIELD:	6 ½ dozen
PORTIONS:	78 cookies
PORTION SIZE:	1 oz (28 g)

10 oz	Margarine, softened	280 g
3 oz	Sugar	80 g
2 oz	Orange juice	57 g
3 oz	Eggs	80 g
11 oz	Molasses, light	320 g
8 oz	Skim milk	220 g
1 lb 10 oz	Pastry flour	750 g
¼ oz	Baking soda	7 g
¼ oz	Cinnamon	7 g
1 lb	Raisins, dark seedless Grated peel of 2 oranges	460 g
5 lb	Total weight	2260 g

Nutritional Information per Serving

	Amount	Calories
Calories		114
Fat	3 g	27
Saturated fatty acid	<1 g	6
Cholesterol	5 mg	
Carbohydrate	21 g	
Added sugars	10 g	
Fiber	1 g	
Protein	1 g	
Sodium	64 mg	
Potassium	103 mg	
Vitamin A	40 RE	
Vitamin C	1 mg	
Calcium	17 mg	
Iron	1 mg	

PROCEDURE

1. Cream together margarine, sugar, juice, eggs, molasses, and milk until light and fluffy.

2. Sift together flour, baking soda, and cinnamon. Stir into creamed mixture.

3. Fold in orange peel and raisins.

4. Portion 78 1 oz (28 g) cookies onto parchment-lined sheet pans.

5. Bake 350° F (175° C) for 12 to 15 minutes. Remove cookies to wire rack and cool.

6. When they are cool, dip cookies into glaze just to cover tops.

Glaze

14 oz	Confectioners' sugar	400 g
4 oz	Orange juice Grated peel of 2 oranges	120 g

Beat until smooth.

STRAWBERRY BARS

YIELD:	1 sheet pan, 18 × 26 in (46 × 66 cm)
PORTIONS:	60 bars
PORTION SIZE:	1 ½ oz (43 g)

Nutritional Information per Serving		
	Amount	*Calories*
Calories		132
Fat	6 g	54
Saturated fatty acid	<1 g	4
Cholesterol	8 mg	
Carbohydrate	19 g	
Added sugars	9 g	
Fiber	1 g	
Protein	2 g	
Sodium	41 mg	
Potassium	62 mg	
Vitamin A	4 RE	
Vitamin C	6 mg	
Calcium	11 mg	
Iron	<1 mg	

	6 oz	Eggs	170 g
	8 oz	Egg whites	230 g
	12 oz	Oil	340 g
	8 oz	Buttermilk	230 g
	12 oz	Pastry flour	340 g
	12 oz	Whole wheat pastry flour	340 g
1 lb	4 oz	Sugar	560 g
	2 tsp	Baking soda	10 g
	2 tsp	Cinnamon	15 g
1 lb	8 oz	Strawberries, fresh, finely chopped*	680 g
6 lb	6 oz	Total weight	2915 g

* If using frozen, unsweetened strawberries, thaw slightly, chop, drain, and weigh.

PROCEDURE

1. Combine eggs, egg whites, oil, and buttermilk.

2. Beat in flours, sugar, baking soda, and cinnamon.

3. Carefully stir in strawberries.

4. Spread batter into a lightly greased 18 × 26 in (46 × 66 cm) sheet pan.

5. Bake at 350° F (175° C) for 25 to 35 minutes or until bars spring back in middle when touched.

SOUR CREAM BROWNIES

YIELD:	1 sheet pan, 18 × 26 in (46 × 66 cm)
PORTIONS:	72
PORTION SIZE:	2 oz (57 g)

12 oz		Egg whites	340 g
2 lb		Sugar	900 g
2 lb		Lowfat sour cream,	
		(2 g fat per oz)	900 g
	1 oz	Vanilla	28 g
	10 oz	Pastry flour	280 g
	10 oz	Whole wheat pastry flour	280 g
	10 oz	Cocoa	280 g
	1/2 oz	Baking powder	14 g
	1 tsp	Baking soda	5 g
	8 oz	Walnuts, chopped	230 g
7 lb	4 oz	Total weight	3257 g

Nutritional Information per Serving

	Amount	Calories
Calories		161
Fat	5 g	45
Saturated fatty acid	1 g	9
Cholesterol	0 mg	
Carbohydrate	29 g	
Added sugars	19 g	
Fiber	2 g	
Protein	4 g	
Sodium	69 mg	
Potassium	107 mg	
Vitamin A	30 RE	
Vitamin C	<1 mg	
Calcium	34 mg	
Iron	1 mg	

PROCEDURE

1. Beat egg whites, sugar, sour cream, and vanilla until well blended.

2. Add flours, cocoa, baking powder, and baking soda.

3. Stir in walnuts.

4. Spread batter into a lightly greased 18 × 26 in (46 × 66 cm) sheet pan.

5. Bake at 350° F (175° C) for 22 to 25 minutes or until done. Cool. Ice.

Icing

1 lb		Confectioners sugar	450 g
	3 oz	Cocoa	85 g
	3 oz	Margarine, unsalted, room temperature	85 g
	4 oz	Skim milk	110 g
	1/2 oz	Vanilla	14 g

Beat all ingredients until smooth.

CHEESECAKE BARS

YIELD:	1 sheet pan, 18 × 26 in (46 × 66 cm)
PORTIONS:	72
PORTION SIZE:	2 oz (57 g)

Nutritional Information per Serving		
	Amount	Calories
Calories		150
Fat	7 g	63
Saturated fatty acid	3 g	27
Cholesterol	15 mg	
Carbohydrate	19 g	
Added sugars	9 g	
Fiber	1 g	
Protein	4 g	
Sodium	117 mg	
Potassium	76 mg	
Vitamin A	83 RE	
Vitamin C	1 mg	
Calcium	34 mg	
Iron	1 mg	

1 lb		Pastry flour	450 g
	10 oz	Whole wheat flour	280 g
	12 oz	Brown sugar	340 g
	6 oz	Margarine	170 g
	4 oz	Water	110 g
3 lb		Neufchatel cheese	1360 g
1 lb		Lowfat sour cream (2 g fat per oz)	450 g
	12 oz	Sugar	340 g
	12 oz	Egg whites	340 g
	8 oz	Skim milk	230 g
	3 oz	Lemon juice	85 g
	1 oz	Vanilla	28 g
9 lb	4 oz	Total weight	4183 g

PROCEDURE

1. Combine flours and brown sugar. Cut in margarine. Stir in water.

2. Pat dough into a lightly greased 18 × 26 in (46 × 66 cm) sheet pan.

3. Bake at 350° F (175° C) for 8 minutes.

4. Beat together remaining ingredients to a smooth batter.

5. Pour into prebaked crust.

6. Bake 30 to 35 minutes or until edges begin to brown and middle is firm.

MARBLE CHEESECAKE BARS

YIELD:	1 sheet pan, 18 × 26 in (46 × 66 cm)
PORTIONS:	72
PORTION SIZE:	2 oz (57 g)

2 lb		Lowfat ricotta cheese	
		(1 g fat per oz)	900 g
	10 oz	Egg whites	280 g
	8 oz	Sugar	230 g
	6 oz	Pastry flour	170 g
	1 oz	Vanilla	28 g
1 lb		Buttermilk	450 g
	10 oz	Margarine, unsalted, melted	280 g
	12 oz	Egg whites	340 g
	1 oz	Vanilla	28 g
1 lb	2 oz	Pastry flour	500 g
1 lb	8 oz	Sugar	680 g
	6 oz	Cocoa	170 g
	2½ tsp	Baking soda	12 g
9 lb		Total weight	4068 g

Nutritional Information per Serving

	Amount	Calories
Calories		136
Fat	4 g	36
Saturated fatty acid	1 g	9
Cholesterol	2 mg	
Carbohydrate	22 g	
Added sugars	12 g	
Fiber	1 g	
Protein	4 g	
Sodium	97 mg	
Potassium	78 mg	
Vitamin A	54 RE	
Vitamin C	<1 mg	
Calcium	30 mg	
Iron	1 mg	

PROCEDURE

1. Mix first five ingredients and beat until smooth. Set aside.
2. Combine buttermilk, margarine, egg whites, and vanilla.
3. Add pastry flour, sugar, cocoa, and baking soda.
4. Spoon this batter into a lightly greased 18 × 26 in (46 × 66 cm) sheet pan.
5. Deposit pools of first batter over batter in pan and swirl with a knife.
6. Bake at 350° F (175° C) 35 to 40 minutes or until firm.

PUMPKIN BARS

YIELD: 6 dozen
PORTIONS: 72
PORTION SIZE: 2 oz (57 g)

Nutritional Information per Serving		
	Amount	*Calories*
Calories		147
Fat	5 g	45
Saturated fatty acid	1 g	9
Cholesterol	<1 mg	
Carbohydrate	25 g	
Added sugars	8 g	
Fiber	1 g	
Protein	2 g	
Sodium	142 mg	
Potassium	128 mg	
Vitamin A	278 RE	
Vitamin C	1 mg	
Calcium	23 mg	
Iron	1 mg	

	13 ½ oz	Margarine, softened	380 g
1 lb	5 oz	Sugar	600 g
1 lb	3 oz	Buttermilk	540 g
	14 oz	Egg whites	400 g
	½ oz	Vanilla	14 g
1 lb	10 oz	Pumpkin, canned	740 g
1 lb	10 oz	Pastry flour	740 g
	⅓ oz	Baking soda	10 g
	1 oz	Cocoa	30 g
	¼ oz	Allspice	7 g
	¼ oz	Cinnamon	7 g
	¼ oz	Cloves	7 g
	¼ oz	Nutmeg	7 g
	¼ oz	Salt	7 g
1 lb	7 oz	Raisins, dark seedless	650 g
9 lb		Total weight	4139 g

PROCEDURE

1. Combine margarine, sugar, buttermilk, egg whites, vanilla, and pumpkin. Mix thoroughly.

2. Add dry ingredients and mix until moistened.

3. Soak raisins in 8 oz (227 g) water for 5 minutes. Fold into batter.

4. Spread into lightly greased 18 × 26 in (46 × 66 cm) sheet pan.

5. Bake at 350° F (175° C) 30 to 40 minutes or until toothpick inserted into center comes out clean.

RASPBERRY-FUDGE BARS

YIELD:	1 sheet pan, 18 × 26 in (46 × 66 cm)
PORTIONS:	72
PORTION SIZE:	2 oz (57 g)

1 lb	12 oz		Sugar	800 g
1 lb			Oil	450 g
1 lb			Egg whites	450 g
		¾ oz	Vanilla	21 g
	12 oz		Pastry flour	340 g
	12 oz		Whole wheat pastry flour	340 g
	8 oz		Cocoa	230 g
	¼ oz		Baking soda	7 g
2 lb			Buttermilk	900 g
1 lb	4 oz		Raspberry jam, melted	560 g
9 lb	1 oz		Total weight	4098 g

Nutritional Information per Serving		
	Amount	*Calories*
Calories		169
Fat	7 g	63
Saturated fatty acid	<1 g	4
Cholesterol	<1 mg	
Carbohydrate	26 g	
Added sugars	11 g	
Fiber	2 g	
Protein	3 g	
Sodium	53 mg	
Potassium	96 mg	
Vitamin A	1 RE	
Vitamin C	<1 mg	
Calcium	24 mg	
Iron	1 mg	

PROCEDURE

1. Beat sugar, oil, egg whites, and vanilla until light.
2. Combine flours, cocoa, and baking soda.
3. Add oil mixture to flour alternately with buttermilk.
4. Spread batter into a lightly greased 18 × 26 in (46 × 66 cm) sheet pan.
5. Drizzle jam over top of batter.
6. Bake at 375° F (190° C) for 22 to 25 minutes.

APPLE BARS

YIELD:	1 sheet pan, 18 × 26 in (46 × 66 cm)
PORTIONS:	72
PORTION SIZE:	2 ½ oz (70 g)

Nutritional Information per Serving		
	Amount	*Calories*
Calories		192
Fat	7 g	63
Saturated fatty acid	<1 g	4
Cholesterol	14 mg	
Carbohydrate	31 g	
Added sugars	20 g	
Fiber	1 g	
Protein	3 g	
Sodium	78 mg	
Potassium	66 mg	
Vitamin A	8 RE	
Vitamin C	<1 mg	
Calcium	22 mg	
Iron	1 mg	

2 lb		Sugar	900 g
1 lb		Oil	450 g
	8 oz	Eggs	230 g
	8 oz	Egg whites	230 g
1 lb	4 oz	Bread flour	560 g
	12 oz	Whole wheat flour	340 g
	½ oz	Baking soda	14 g
	¼ oz	Cinnamon	7 g
2 lb		Buttermilk	900 g
2 lb		Apples, water-packed, drained, chopped	900 g
10 lb	1 oz	Total weight	4531 g

PROCEDURE

1. Beat sugar, oil, eggs, and egg whites until light.

2. Combine flours, baking soda, and cinnamon.

3. Add oil mixture to flour alternately with buttermilk.

4. Stir in apples.

5. Spread batter into a lightly greased 18 × 26 in (46 × 66 cm) sheet pan.

6. Bake at 375° F (190° C) for 30 to 35 minutes or until done. Cool. Ice.

Icing

1 lb		Confectioners' sugar	450 g
	2 oz	Maple syrup	55 g

Beat sugar and maple syrup with enough hot water to make a spreadable icing.

FRUIT BARS

YIELD:	1 sheet pan, 18 × 26 in (46 × 66 cm)
PORTIONS:	72
PORTION SIZE:	2 oz (57 g)

2 lb		Oats, quick	900 g
	12 oz	Brown sugar	340 g
	8 oz	Pastry flour	230 g
	8 oz	Whole wheat flour	230 g
	8 oz	Margarine	230 g
	8 oz	Apple juice concentrate, thawed	230 g
4 lb	4 oz	Fruit pie filling	1900 g
9 lb		Total weight	4060 g

Nutritional Information per Serving		
	Amount	*Calories*
Calories		146
Fat	4 g	36
Saturated fatty acid	<1 g	5
Cholesterol	0 mg	
Carbohydrate	26 g	
Added sugars	5 g	
Fiber	2 g	
Protein	3 g	
Sodium	41 mg	
Potassium	119 mg	
Vitamin A	33 RE	
Vitamin C	<1 mg	
Calcium	20 mg	
Iron	1 mg	

PROCEDURE

1. Combine oats, brown sugar, and flours. Cut in margarine and juice concentrate.

2. Firmly press one-half of mixture into a lightly greased 18 × 26 in (46 × 66 cm) sheet pan.

3. Spread pie filling evenly over crust.

4. Sprinkle remaining mixture over filling. Lightly press down.

5. Bake at 375° F (190° C) for 30 to 35 minutes or until topping is golden brown.

DATE BARS

YIELD:	1 sheet pan, 18 × 26 in (46 × 66 cm)
PORTIONS:	72
PORTION SIZE:	2 oz (57 g)

Nutritional Information per Serving		
	Amount	Calories
Calories		166
Fat	4 g	36
Saturated fatty acid	<1 g	6
Cholesterol	0 mg	
Carbohydrate	33 g	
Added sugars	5 g	
Fiber	3 g	
Protein	3 g	
Sodium	34 mg	
Potassium	214 mg	
Vitamin A	34 RE	
Vitamin C	2 mg	
Calcium	21 mg	
Iron	1 mg	

2 lb	12 oz	Dates, chopped	1250 g
	12 oz	Orange juice	340 g
	12 oz	Water	340 g
2 lb		Oats, quick	900 g
	12 oz	Brown sugar	340 g
	8 oz	Pastry flour	230 g
	8 oz	Whole wheat flour	230 g
	8 oz	Margarine	230 g
	8 oz	Apple juice concentrate, thawed	230 g
9 lb		Total weight	4090 g

PROCEDURE

1. Combine dates, orange juice, and water in a saucepan. Cook slowly until dates soften and liquids are absorbed, stirring often. Cool.

2. Combine oats, brown sugar, and flours. Cut in margarine and juice concentrate.

3. Firmly press one-half of mixture into a lightly greased 18 × 26 in (46 × 66 cm) sheet pan.

4. Spread date filling evenly over crust.

5. Sprinkle remaining mixture over filling. Lightly press down.

6. Bake at 375° F (190° C) for 30 to 35 minutes or until topping is golden brown.

10   CAKES

Cakes are one of the most adaptable desserts. In this chapter their versatility is demonstrated by a variety of sponge cakes, layer cakes, upside-down cakes, cupcakes, pudding cakes, and even cheesecakes. Although cakes usually contain a larger proportion of fat and sugar, our formulas have been reduced in fat and sugar, but not in taste.

Large-quantity cake formulas frequently incorporate mixes, as ease in preparation is a significant factor. This chapter presents formulas that will meet your need for quick and easy preparation in quantity.

Many of these cakes are un-iced to limit the sugar and fat contents, but some have a light glaze or fruit sauce to provide visual appeal.

FORMULAS

Chocolate-Applesauce Cake	*Applesauce Picnic Cake*
Cocoa-Mint Angel Food Cake	*Cocoa Chiffon Cake*
Gingerbread with Lemon Sauce	*White Cake*
Pound Cake	*Spice Cake*
Prune Cake	*Fruit Flan*
Sponge Cake	*Chocolate-Cherry Torte*
Apple Kuchen	*Cocoa-Bean Cake*
Chocolate Pudding Cake	*Lemon Chiffon Cheesecake*
Double Chocolate Cupcakes	*Peanut Squares*
Pineapple Upside-Down Cake	*Carrot Cake with Creamy*
Chocolate Cake with Meringue	*Frosting*
Icing	

CHOCOLATE-APPLESAUCE CAKE

YIELD: 1 sheet pan, 18 × 26 in (46 × 66 cm)
PORTIONS: 72
PORTION SIZE: 2 oz (57 g)

Nutritional Information per Serving		
	Amount	*Calories*
Calories		178
Fat	7 g	63
Saturated fatty acid	1 g	9
Cholesterol	0 mg	
Carbohydrate	28 g	
Added sugars	16 g	
Fiber	2.5 g	
Protein	3 g	
Sodium	118 mg	
Potassium	102 mg	
Vitamin A	1 RE	
Vitamin C	<1 mg	
Calcium	17 mg	
Iron	1 mg	

2 lb		Sugar	900 g
1 lb	4 oz	Pastry flour	550 g
	12 oz	Whole wheat pastry flour	340 g
	7 oz	Cocoa	200 g
	1 oz	Baking soda	28 g
	2 tbsp	Cinnamon	9 g
2 lb	8 oz	Applesauce, unsweetened	1130 g
	12 oz	Egg whites	340 g
	12 oz	Oil	340 g
	1 oz	Vanilla	28 g
	6 oz	Almonds, chopped	170 g
9 lb		Total weight	4035 g

PROCEDURE

1. Combine sugar, flours, cocoa, baking soda, and cinnamon.

2. Beat together applesauce, egg whites, oil, and vanilla.

3. Stir wet ingredients into flour mixture, and blend thoroughly.

4. Spread batter into a lightly greased 18 × 26 in (46 × 66 cm) sheet pan.

5. Sprinkle almonds over batter.

6. Bake at 350° F (175° C) for 25 to 35 minutes or until cake springs back when lightly touched.

7. Drizzle chocolate glaze over warm cake.

Chocolate Glaze

6 oz	Confectioners' sugar	170 g
1 oz	Cocoa	28 g
2 oz	Corn syrup	55 g
2 oz	Hot water	55 g

Beat all ingredients until smooth.

COCOA-MINT ANGEL FOOD CAKE

YIELD:	Three 10 in (25 cm) tube cakes
PORTIONS:	36 (12 servings per cake)
PORTION SIZE:	2⅖ oz (67 g)

Nutritional Information per Serving		
	Amount	Calories
Calories		141
Fat	0 g	0
Saturated fatty acid	0 g	0
Cholesterol	0 mg	
Carbohydrate	31 g	
Added sugars	22 g	
Fiber	1 g	
Protein	4 g	
Sodium	57 mg	
Potassium	77 mg	
Vitamin A	<1 RE	
Vitamin C	<1 mg	
Calcium	7 mg	
Iron	1 mg	

2 lb	4 oz	Egg whites	1020 g
	¼ oz	Cream of tartar	7 g
	14 oz	Sugar	400 g
	½ oz	Vanilla	14 g
	14 oz	Sugar	400 g
	9 oz	Cake flour	250 g
	4 oz	Cocoa	110 g
	6 oz	Peppermint candies, crushed	170 g
5 lb	4 oz	Total weight	2371 g

PROCEDURE

1. Whip egg whites with cream of tartar until foamy.

2. Slowly add 14 oz (400 g) sugar while whipping to medium peaks.

3. Whip in vanilla.

4. Sift second 14 oz (400 g) sugar, flour, and cocoa twice.

5. Fold flour mixture into egg whites. Fold in candies.

6. Scale 1 lb 12 oz (790 g) batter into each of three 10 in (25 cm) tube pans.

7. Bake at 350° F (175 ° C) for 45 to 50 minutes or until cake springs back when lightly touched. Cool inverted.

GINGERBREAD WITH LEMON SAUCE

YIELD:	1 sheet pan, 18 × 26 in (46 × 66 cm)
PORTIONS:	60
PORTION SIZE:	3 oz (85 g)

		Ingredient	
1 lb		Molasses	450 g
	12 oz	Oil	340 g
	12 oz	Brown sugar	340 g
1 lb	8 oz	Buttermilk	680 g
	8 oz	Eggs	230 g
	4 oz	Egg whites	110 g
	1 oz	Baking soda	28 g
1 lb	4 oz	Pastry flour	560 g
	12 oz	Rye flour, dark	340 g
	½ oz	Ginger	14 g
	¼ oz	Cinnamon	7 g
6 lb	14 oz	Total weight	3099 g

PROCEDURE

1. Beat together molasses, oil, and brown sugar.

2. Add buttermilk, eggs, egg whites, and baking soda, and mix until smooth.

3. Stir in flours and spices.

4. Spread batter into a lightly greased 18 × 26 in (46 × 66 cm) sheet pan.

5. Bake at 350° F (175 ° C) for 25 to 30 minutes or until cake springs back when lightly touched. Serve warm or cool.

6. Cut cake into 60 servings; spoon 1 oz (28 g)—2 tbsp—lemon sauce over each cake portion.

Lemon Sauce

		Ingredient	
2 lb	4 oz	Water	1000 g
	8 oz	Sugar	230 g
	2½ oz	Cornstarch	75 g
	12 oz	Lemon juice	340 g
	1½ oz	Grated lemon rind	43 g

1. Cook water, sugar, and cornstarch over medium heat until thickened.

2. Remove from heat. Add lemon juice and rind. Add yellow food color, if desired.

Nutritional Information per Serving		
	Amount	*Calories*
Calories		192
Fat	6 g	54
Saturated fatty acid	1 g	9
Cholesterol	17 mg	
Carbohydrate	31 g	
Added sugars	18 g	
Fiber	2 g	
Protein	3 g	
Sodium	154 mg	
Potassium	170 mg	
Vitamin A	9 RE	
Vitamin C	4 mg	
Calcium	40 mg	
Iron	1 mg	

POUND CAKE

YIELD: 6 loaves, 1 lb 4 oz (560 g) each
PORTIONS: 60 servings (10 servings per loaf)
PORTION SIZE: 2 oz (57 g)

		Nutritional Information per Serving		

<table>
<tr><td colspan="3">Nutritional Information per Serving</td></tr>
<tr><td></td><td>Amount</td><td>Calories</td></tr>
<tr><td>Calories</td><td></td><td>168</td></tr>
<tr><td>Fat</td><td>6 g</td><td>54</td></tr>
<tr><td>Saturated fatty acid</td><td>1 g</td><td>9</td></tr>
<tr><td>Cholesterol</td><td>1 mg</td><td></td></tr>
<tr><td>Carbohydrate</td><td>25 g</td><td></td></tr>
<tr><td>Added sugars</td><td>9 g</td><td></td></tr>
<tr><td>Fiber</td><td>1 g</td><td></td></tr>
<tr><td>Protein</td><td>3 g</td><td></td></tr>
<tr><td>Sodium</td><td>156 mg</td><td></td></tr>
<tr><td>Potassium</td><td>66 mg</td><td></td></tr>
<tr><td>Vitamin A</td><td>77 RE</td><td></td></tr>
<tr><td>Vitamin C</td><td><1 mg</td><td></td></tr>
<tr><td>Calcium</td><td>33 mg</td><td></td></tr>
<tr><td>Iron</td><td>1 mg</td><td></td></tr>
</table>

1 lb	4 oz	Sugar		560 g
1 lb		Margarine		450 g
	2 oz	Vanilla		55 g
	12 oz	Egg whites		340 g
2 lb	6 oz	Cake flour		1070 g
	½ oz	Baking soda		14 g
2 lb		Yogurt, low-fat, plain		900 g
7 lb	8 oz	Total weight		3389 g

PROCEDURE

1. Cream sugar, margarine, and vanilla. Stir in egg whites gradually.
2. Combine flour and baking soda.
3. Beat flour mixture into creamed mixture alternately with the yogurt, taking care not to overmix.
4. Lightly grease six 7⅜ × 3⅝ in (19 × 9 cm) loaf pans.
5. Scale 1 lb 4 oz (560 g) batter into each loaf pan.
6. Bake at 350° F (175 ° C) for 45 to 55 minutes or until cake is golden and firm.

PRUNE CAKE

YIELD: 1 half-sheet pan, 13 × 18 in (33 × 46 cm)
PORTIONS: 45
PORTION SIZE: 2 oz (57 g)

Nutritional Information per Serving		
	Amount	*Calories*
Calories		173
Fat	7 g	63
Saturated fatty acid	1 g	9
Cholesterol	<1 mg	
Carbohydrate	27 g	
Added sugars	11 g	
Fiber	2 g	
Protein	2 g	
Sodium	90 mg	
Potassium	153 mg	
Vitamin A	40 RE	
Vitamin C	1 mg	
Calcium	33 mg	
Iron	1 mg	

	12 oz	Brown sugar	340 g
	8 oz	Oil	230 g
	6 oz	Egg whites	170 g
	½ oz	Vanilla	14 g
1 lb	3 oz	Buttermilk	540 g
	12 oz	Pastry flour	340 g
	6 oz	Whole wheat pastry flour	170 g
	¼ oz	Baking soda	7 g
	1 ½ tsp	Cinnamon	2 g
	1 ½ tsp	Nutmeg	3 g
1 lb		Prunes, finely chopped	450 g
5 lb		Total weight	2266 g

PROCEDURE

1. Beat brown sugar, oil, egg whites and vanilla. Add buttermilk.
2. Stir in flours, baking soda, and spices until blended.
3. Stir in prunes.
4. Spread batter into a lightly greased 13 × 18 in (33 × 46 cm) sheet pan.
5. Bake at 350° F (175 ° C) for 25 to 30 minutes or until cake springs back when lightly touched.
6. Spread warm glaze over hot cake. Cool before serving.

Glaze

6 oz	Sugar	170 g
3 oz	Margarine, unsalted	85 g
3 oz	Buttermilk	85 g
¼ tsp	Baking soda	1 g
½ oz	Vanilla	14 g

Cook all ingredients except vanilla over low heat until thickened and golden brown, about 5 to 10 minutes. Add vanilla. Use immediately.

SPONGE CAKE

YIELD:	Four 10 in (25 cm) tube cakes
PORTIONS:	48 (12 servings per cake)
PORTION SIZE:	2 ⅖ oz (67 g)

Nutritional Information per Serving		
	Amount	Calories
Calories		162
Fat	2 g	18
Saturated fatty acid	<1 g	4
Cholesterol	71 mg	
Carbohydrate	33 g	
Added sugars	21 g	
Fiber	<1 g	
Protein	4 g	
Sodium	51 mg	
Potassium	68 mg	
Vitamin A	33 RE	
Vitamin C	4 mg	
Calcium	15 mg	
Iron	1 mg	

10 oz	Egg yolks	280 g
1 lb	Orange juice	450 g
1 lb 12 oz	Sugar	800 g
1 oz	Vanilla	28 g
1 lb 8oz	Cake flour	680 g
½ oz	Baking powder	14 g
1 lb 8 oz	Egg whites	680 g
2 tsp	Cream of tartar	4 g
8 oz	Sugar	230 g
7 lb	Total weight	3166 g

PROCEDURE

1. Whip egg yolks until thick, about 5 minutes. Add orange juice.
2. Gradually add 1 lb 12 oz sugar and vanilla and whip until doubled. Set aside.
3. Sift cake flour and baking powder.
4. Whip egg whites with cream of tartar until foamy.
5. Gradually add 8 oz (230 g) sugar and whip to firm peaks.
6. Fold flour mixture into egg yolks mixture.
7. Carefully fold in egg whites.
8. Scale 1 lb 12 oz (790 g) batter into each of four 10 in (25 cm) tube pans.
9. Bake at 350° F (175° C) for 35 to 45 minutes or until cake springs back when lightly touched. Cool inverted.

APPLE KUCHEN

YIELD:	Six 10 in (25 cm) cakes *or* 1 sheet pan, 18 × 26 in (46 × 66 cm)
PORTIONS:	60 (10 servings per cake if using 10 in [25 cm] pans)
PORTION SIZE:	3 oz (90 g)

Nutritional Information per Serving

	Amount	Calories
Calories		194
Fat	5 g	45
Saturated fatty acid	1 g	9
Cholesterol	<1 g	
Carbohydrate	35 g	
Added sugars	11 g	
Fiber	2 g	
Protein	4 g	
Sodium	133 mg	
Potassium	98 mg	
Vitamin A	58 RE	
Vitamin C	1 mg	
Calcium	25 mg	
Iron	1 mg	

Streusel

1 lb	2 oz	Pastry flour	500 g
	12 oz	Sugar	340 g
	6 oz	Margarine	170 g
2 lb	4 oz	Total weight	1010 g

Cake

1 lb	4 oz	Pastry flour	560 g
	12 oz	Whole wheat pastry flour	340 g
	12 oz	Sugar	340 g
	1¼ oz	Baking powder	35 g
	6 oz	Margarine	170 g
	12 oz	Egg whites	340 g
	8 oz	Buttermilk	230 g
	1½ oz	Vanilla	42 g

Filling

4 lb	8 oz	Apples, fresh, peeled, cored thinly sliced	2050 g
9 lb		Total weight	4107 g

FOR STREUSEL

Combine sugar and pastry flour. Cut in margarine.

FOR CAKE

1. Combine flours, sugar, and baking powder. Cut in margarine.
2. Beat together egg whites, buttermilk, and vanilla.
3. Stir wet ingredients into flour mixture to make a stiff dough.
4. Press dough into a lightly greased 18 × 26 in (46 × 66 cm) sheet pan, *or* scale 12 oz (340 g) dough into each of six 10 in (25 cm) lightly greased cake pans.
5. Gently press dough ½ inch (1.25 cm) up sides of pans.
6. Place apple slices over dough, using 12 oz (340 g) apples per 10 in (25 cm) cake.
7. Sprinkle streusel over apples, using 8 oz (230 g) streusel per 10 in (25 cm) cake.
8. Bake at 350° F (175 ° C) for 35 minutes or until apples are tender and cake is done.

CHOCOLATE PUDDING CAKE

YIELD: 1 sheet pan, 18 × 26 in (46 × 66 cm)
PORTIONS: 32
PORTION SIZE: 4 oz (113 g)

	14 oz	Pastry flour	400 g
	14 oz	Sugar	400 g
	1½ oz	Cocoa	40 g
	1 oz	Baking powder	30 g
1 lb	1 oz	Skim milk	490 g
	3 oz	Oil	80 g
	½ oz	Vanilla	14 g
	4 oz	Walnuts, chopped	120 g
1 lb	4 oz	Brown sugar	570 g
	3 oz	Cocoa	80 g
3 lb	8 oz	Water, hot	1590 g
8 lb	6 oz	Total weight	3810 g

PROCEDURE

1. Sift together flour, sugar, cocoa, and baking powder.

2. Add milk, oil, and vanilla; mix until smooth.

3. Stir in walnuts.

4. Pour batter into a lightly greased 18 × 26 in (46 × 66 cm) sheet pan with 2 in (5 cm) extenders.

5. Mix brown sugar and cocoa; sprinkle over batter.

6. Pour hot water over batter.

7. Bake at 350° F (175° C) about 45 minutes or until cake springs when touched lightly. Cool cake before cutting. Pudding on the bottom of the cake can be spooned over each piece when serving.

Nutritional Information per Serving		
	Amount	Calories
Calories		221
Fat	6 g	54
Saturated fatty acid	1 g	9
Cholesterol	<1 mg	
Carbohydrate	43 g	
Added sugars	30 g	
Fiber	1 g	
Protein	3 g	
Sodium	114 mg	
Potassium	163 mg	
Vitamin A	10 RE	
Vitamin C	<1 mg	
Calcium	62 mg	
Iron	2 mg	

DOUBLE CHOCOLATE CUPCAKES

YIELD: 3 dozen
PORTIONS: 36
PORTION SIZE: 2 oz (57 g)

Nutritional Information per Serving		
	Amount	*Calories*
Calories		166
Fat	6 g	54
Saturated fatty acid	2 g	18
Cholesterol	0 mg	
Carbohydrate	28 g	
Added sugars	10 g	
Fiber	1 g	
Protein	3 g	
Sodium	186 mg	
Potassium	107 mg	
Vitamin A	1 RE	
Vitamin C	4 mg	
Calcium	11 mg	
Iron	1 mg	

1 lb	1½ oz	Pastry flour	500 g
	9 oz	Whole wheat flour	270 g
	15½ oz	Sugar	440 g
	4¼ oz	Cocoa powder	120 g
	⅝ oz	Baking soda	19 g
	⅛ oz	Salt	4 g
	12½ oz	Water	350 g
1 lb	1½ oz	Orange juice	500 g
	5 oz	Oil	150 g
	2½ oz	Vinegar	70 g
	2½ oz	Vanilla	70 g
	8 oz	Chocolate chips, semisweet	225 ml
6 lb		Total weight	2718 g

PROCEDURE

1. Combine flours, sugar, cocoa, baking soda, and salt in mixing bowl.
2. Add remaining ingredients, except for chocolate chips.
3. Mix until ingredients are just moistened.
4. Fold in chocolate chips.
5. Portion 2 oz (57 g) batter into each of 36 paper-lined muffin cups.
6. Bake at 375° F (190° C) for 12 to 15 minutes or until a wooden pick inserted into center of cupcake comes out clean.

PINEAPPLE UPSIDE-DOWN CAKE

YIELD:	1 cake pan, 12 × 20 in (30 × 50 cm)
PORTIONS:	36
PORTION SIZE:	3 ½ oz (99 g)

Nutritional Information per Serving		
	Amount	Calories
Calories		196
Fat	4 g	36
Saturated fatty acid	1 g	9
Cholesterol	15 mg	
Carbohydrate	37 g	
Added sugars	17 g	
Fiber	1 g	
Protein	2 g	
Sodium	226 mg	
Potassium	126 mg	
Vitamin A	61 RE	
Vitamin C	5 mg	
Calcium	50 mg	
Iron	1 mg	

3 lb	1 oz	Pineapple rings in unsweetened juice, drained (reserve juice)	1390 g
	2 oz	Margarine, melted	57 g
	7¾ oz	Brown sugar	220 g
	9 oz	Pineapple juice (reserved from pineapple rings)	250 g
	3½ oz	Eggs	100 g
	3½ oz	Egg whites	100 g
	14 oz	Sugar	400 g
	4 oz	Margarine, melted	113 g
1 lb	4 oz	Pastry flour, sifted	575 g
	1 oz	Baking powder	20 g
	¼ oz	Salt	5 g
1 lb	1 oz	Skim milk	490 g
	1½ oz	Vanilla	40 g
8 lb	4 oz	Total weight	3760 g

PROCEDURE

1. Combine 2 oz (57 g) margarine and brown sugar in saucepan; cook over medium heat 1 minute.
2. Add reserved pineapple juice; cook 1 more minute, stirring constantly.
3. Spread mixture evenly into a 12 × 20 in (30 × 50 cm) pan.
4. Arrange pineapple slices in a single layer over brown sugar mixture.
5. Beat eggs until foamy; gradually add sugar and melted margarine.
6. Combine flour, baking powder, and salt. Add to sugar mixture alternately with milk, beginning and ending with flour mixture. Mix well after each addition.
7. Stir in vanilla.
8. Pour batter over pineapple.
9. Bake at 350° F (175° C) about 45 minutes or until lightly browned.
10. Cool in pan 5 minutes; invert cake.

CHOCOLATE CAKE WITH MERINGUE ICING

YIELD: 1 half-sheet pan, 13 × 18 in (33 × 46 cm)
PORTIONS: 36
PORTION SIZE: 2 ½ oz (70 g)

Nutritional Information per Serving		
	Amount	*Calories*
Calories		169
Fat	6 g	54
Saturated fatty acid	1 g	9
Cholesterol	<1 mg	
Carbohydrate	29 g	
Added sugars	17 g	
Fiber	2 g	
Protein	3 g	
Sodium	241 mg	
Potassium	98 mg	
Vitamin A	1 RE	
Vitamin C	<1 mg	
Calcium	23 mg	
Iron	1 mg	

1 lb	2 oz	Sugar	500 g
	6 oz	Oil	170 g
	4 oz	Egg whites	110 g
	½ oz	Vanilla	14 g
1 lb		Buttermilk	450 g
	8 oz	Pastry flour	230 g
	8 oz	Whole wheat pastry flour	230 g
	4 oz	Cocoa	110 g
	1 oz	Baking soda	28 g
1 lb		Water or coffee, boiling	450 g
5 lb	1 oz	Total weight	2292 g

PROCEDURE

1. Beat together sugar, oil, egg whites, and vanilla. Stir in buttermilk.

2. Combine flours, cocoa, and baking soda.

3. Beat flour mixture into liquid mixture alternately with the boiling water (or coffee).

4. Spread batter into a lightly greased 13 × 18 in (33 × 46 cm) sheet pan.

5. Bake at 350° F(175 ° C) for 25 to 30 minutes or until cake springs back when lightly touched.

6. Spread meringue over hot cake, taking care to seal edges.

7. Return to oven and bake until meringue is golden, about 10 to 15 minutes.

Meringue Icing

4 oz	Egg whites	110 g
¼ tsp	Cream of tartar	½ g
4 oz	Sugar	110 g

1. Whip egg whites with cream of tartar until foamy.

2. Slowly add sugar and whip to firm peaks.

APPLESAUCE PICNIC CAKE

YIELD:	Six 8 in (20 cm) square cakes
PORTIONS:	54 (9 servings per cake)
PORTION SIZE:	2 ⅓ oz (66 g)

Nutritional Information per Serving		
	Amount	Calories
Calories		165
Fat	4 g	36
Saturated fatty acid	1 g	9
Cholesterol	0 mg	
Carbohydrate	30 g	
Added sugars	18 g	
Fiber	1 g	
Protein	3 g	
Sodium	135 mg	
Potassium	101 mg	
Vitamin A	55 RE	
Vitamin C	<1 mg	
Calcium	21 mg	
Iron	1 mg	

1 lb		Sugar	450 g
	8 oz	Margarine	230 g
	6 oz	Molasses	170 g
	½ oz	Vanilla	14 g
	10 oz	Egg whites	280 g
1 lb		Pastry flour	450 g
	12 oz	Whole wheat flour	340 g
	½ oz	Baking soda	14 g
	¼ oz	Cinnamon	7 g
	2 tsp	Nutmeg	3 g
	2 tsp	Cloves	3 g
2 lb		Applesauce, unsweetened	900 g
	6 oz	Water	170 g
6 lb	12 oz	Total weight	3031 g

PROCEDURE

1. Cream sugar, margarine, molasses, and vanilla until light and fluffy.

2. Gradually add egg whites.

3. Combine flours, baking soda, and spices.

4. Combine applesauce and water.

5. Stir dry ingredients into creamed mixture alternately with the applesauce.

6. Scale 18 oz (510 g) batter into each of six 8 in (20 cm) lightly greased square pans.

7. Bake at 350° F (175 ° C) for 25 minutes or until cake springs back when lightly touched. Ice when cool.

Icing

2 oz	Margarine, unsalted	55 g
4 oz	Brown sugar	110 g
4 oz	Evaporated skim milk	110 g
8 oz	Confectioners' sugar	230 g
½ tsp	Vanilla	6 g

1. Melt margarine and brown sugar.

2. Add evaporated milk and cook over low heat for 2 minutes. Cool 15 minutes.

3. Beat in confectioners' sugar and vanilla until smooth. Use immediately.

COCOA CHIFFON CAKE

YIELD:	1 sheet pan, 18 × 26 in (46 × 66 cm)
PORTIONS:	64
PORTION SIZE:	2 oz (57 g)

		Nutritional Information per Serving		
			Amount	Calories
Calories				169
Fat			6 g	54
Saturated fatty acid			1 g	9
Cholesterol			27 mg	
Carbohydrate			28 g	
Added sugars			14 g	
Fiber			1 g	
Protein			3 g	
Sodium			76 mg	
Potassium			61 mg	
Vitamin A			14 RE	
Vitamin C			<1 mg	
Calcium			25 mg	
Iron			1 mg	

1 lb	8 oz	Cake flour	680 g
1 lb	8 oz	Sugar	680 g
	4 oz	Cocoa	110 g
	4 tsp	Baking soda	19 g
	8 oz	Egg whites	230 g
	8 oz	Sugar	230 g
	6 oz	Egg yolks	170 g
	10 oz	Oil	280 g
2 lb		Buttermilk	900 g
7 lb	4 oz	Total weight	3299 g

PROCEDURE

1. Combine dry ingredients. Set aside.

2. Whip egg whites until foamy. Gradually add sugar while whipping to firm peaks.

3. Beat together egg yolks, oil, and buttermilk.

4. Stir dry ingredients into buttermilk mixture.

5. Carefully fold in egg whites.

6. Spread batter into an 18 × 26 in (46 × 66 cm) sheet pan that has been lightly greased on bottom, only.

7. Bake at 350° F (175 ° C) for 30 minutes or until cake springs back when lightly touched.

WHITE CAKE

YIELD: 1 sheet pan, 18 × 26 in (46 × 66 cm)
PORTIONS: 60
PORTION SIZE: 2 oz (57 g)

Nutritional Information per Serving		
	Amount	*Calories*
Calories		137
Fat	3 g	27
Saturated fatty acid	1 g	9
Cholesterol	1 mg	
Carbohydrate	24 g	
Added sugars	13 g	
Fiber	<1 g	
Protein	3 g	
Sodium	140 mg	
Potassium	59 mg	
Vitamin A	39 RE	
Vitamin C	<1 mg	
Calcium	35 mg	
Iron	1 mg	

1 lb		Sugar	450 g
	8 oz	Margarine	230 g
	1 oz	Vanilla	28 g
2 lb	8 oz	Buttermilk	1130 g
2 lb		Cake flour	900 g
	1½ oz	Baking powder	35 g
	2 tsp	Baking soda	10 g
	12 oz	Egg whites	340 g
	12 oz	Sugar	340 g
7 lb	11 oz	Total weight	3463 g

PROCEDURE

1. Cream sugar, margarine, and vanilla. Stir in buttermilk.

2. Combine flour, baking powder, and baking soda.

3. Whip egg whites until foamy. Gradually add sugar while whipping to firm peaks.

4. Beat flour mixture into creamed mixture.

5. Fold in egg whites.

6. Spread batter into a lightly greased 18 × 26 in (46 × 66 cm) sheet pan.

7. Bake at 350° F (175 ° C) for 25 to 30 minutes or until cake springs back when lightly touched.

SPICE CAKE

YIELD:	1 sheet pan, 18 × 26 in (46 × 66 cm)
PORTIONS:	54
PORTION SIZE:	2 oz (57 g)

1 lb	12 oz	Sugar	800 g
1 lb		Margarine	450 g
	½ oz	Vanilla	14 g
	8 oz	Egg whites	230 g
1 lb	12 oz	Cake flour	800 g
	¾ oz	Baking soda	21 g
	2 tsp	Cinnamon	3 g
	2 tsp	Allspice	4 g
2 lb		Buttermilk	900 g
7 lb	1 oz	Total weight	3222 g

PROCEDURES

1. Cream sugar, margarine, and vanilla. Stir in egg whites gradually.

2. Combine flour, baking soda, and spices.

3. Beat flour mixture into creamed mixture alternately with the buttermilk, taking care not to overmix.

4. Spread batter into a lightly greased 18 × 26 in (46 × 66 cm) sheet pan.

5. Bake at 350° F (175 ° C) for 25 to 30 minutes or until cake springs back when lightly touched.

Nutritional Information per Serving		
	Amount	Calories
Calories		180
Fat	7 g	63
Saturated fatty acid	1 g	9
Cholesterol	1 mg	
Carbohydrate	27 g	
Added sugars	15 g	
Fiber	1 g	
Protein	2 g	
Sodium	212 mg	
Potassium	53 mg	
Vitamin A	85 RE	
Vitamin C	<1 mg	
Calcium	27 mg	
Iron	1 mg	

FRUIT FLAN

YIELD:	Four 10 in (25 cm) cakes
PORTIONS:	48 (12 servings per cake)
PORTION SIZE:	3 oz (85 g)

	Sugar	280 g
10 oz	Sugar	280 g
8 oz	Margarine	230 g
6 oz	Eggs	170 g
1 oz	Vanilla	28 g
8 oz	Egg whites	230 g
1 lb 12 oz	Cake flour	800 g
1 oz	Baking powder	28 g
½ oz	Baking soda	14 g
1 lb 6 oz	Buttermilk	620 g
5 lb 4 oz	Total weight	2400 g

Nutritional Information per Serving

	Amount	Calories
Calories		171
Fat	5 g	45
Saturated fatty acid	1 g	9
Cholesterol	16 mg	
Carbohydrate	30 g	
Added sugars	11 g	
Fiber	1 g	
Protein	3 g	
Sodium	218 mg	
Potassium	93 mg	
Vitamin A	55 RE	
Vitamin C	16 mg	
Calcium	38 mg	
Iron	1 mg	

PROCEDURE

1. Cream sugar and margarine until light and fluffy. Beat in eggs and vanilla.
2. Gradually beat in egg whites.
3. Combine flour, baking powder, and baking soda.
4. Stir flour mixture into creamed mixture alternately with the buttermilk.
5. Lightly grease four 10 in (25 cm) flan pans.
6. Spread 1 lb 5 oz (590 g) batter into each pan.
7. Bake at 375° F (190 ° C) for 15 to 20 minutes or until cake springs back when lightly touched. Cool.
8. Glaze cakes with half the apricot glaze.
9. Arrange assorted fruit on cake top. Brush fruit with remaining glaze.

Topping

1 lb 4 oz	Apricot glaze, sugar-free, melted	550 g
3 lb	Fresh fruit	1350 g

CHOCOLATE-CHERRY TORTE

YIELD:	Three 2-layer 8 in (20 cm) tortes
PORTIONS:	48 (16 servings per torte)
PORTION SIZE:	3¾ oz (106 g)

Nutritional Information per Serving		
	Amount	*Calories*
Calories		233
Fat	7 g	63
Saturated fatty acid	1 g	9
Cholesterol	<1 mg	
Carbohydrate	29 g	
Added sugars	18 g	
Fiber	2 g	
Protein	3 g	
Sodium	198 mg	
Potassium	101 mg	
Vitamin A	13 RE	
Vitamin C	<1 mg	
Calcium	29 mg	
Iron	2 mg	

1 lb	10 oz	Cake flour	730 g
1 lb	6 oz	Sugar	620 g
	5 oz	Cocoa	140 g
	1 oz	Baking soda	28 g
	8 oz	Oil	230 g
	6 oz	Egg whites	170 g
1 lb	8 oz	Buttermilk	680 g
	1 oz	Vanilla	28 g
1 lb	8 oz	Boiling water	680 g
7 lb	5 oz	Total weight	3306 g

PROCEDURE

1. Mix flour, sugar, cocoa, and baking soda. Set aside.

2. Stir together oil, egg whites, buttermilk, and vanilla.

3. Beat flour mixture into liquid mixture alternately with the boiling water.

4. Lightly grease six 8 in (20 cm) cake pans and line with parchment circles.

5. Scale 19 oz (540 g) batter into each pan.

6. Bake at 350° F (175° C) for 25 to 30 minutes or until cake springs back when lightly touched. Cool.

7. Place one cake layer on cake board.

8. Spread 8 oz (230 g) cherry pie filling over cake.

9. Top with second cake layer; spread top layer with 8 oz (230 g) cherry pie filling. Repeat for other tortes.

10. Pipe a shell border around torte with icing.

11. Wrap tortes with cellophane cake wrap.

Filling

3 lb	Cherry pie filling	1350 g

Icing

2 oz	Cake shortening	55 g
2 oz	Margarine, unsalted	55 g
12 oz	Confectioners' sugar	340 g
½ oz	Skim milk	14 g
½ oz	Vanilla	14 g

1. Cream shortening and margarine.
2. Add sugar, milk, and vanilla and beat until smooth and light, adding more milk if icing is too stiff.

COCOA-BEAN CAKE

YIELD:	1 sheet pan, 18 × 26 in (46 × 66 cm)
PORTIONS:	50
PORTION SIZE:	2 oz (57 g)

Nutritional Information per Serving		
	Amount	Calories
Calories		141
Fat	5 g	45
Saturated fatty acid	1 g	9
Cholesterol	20 mg	
Carbohydrate	23 g	
Added sugars	12 g	
Fiber	2 g	
Protein	3 g	
Sodium	137 mg	
Potassium	132 mg	
Vitamin A	33 RE	
Vitamin C	<1 mg	
Calcium	37 mg	
Iron	1 mg	

1 lb	6 oz	Pinto beans, canned, with liquid	625 g
	4 oz	Margarine	113 g
	2 oz	Oil	70 g
	3 oz	Cocoa	85 g
1 lb	1 oz	Skim milk	480 g
	½ oz	Baking soda	14 g
	9 oz	Buttermilk	255 g
	7 oz	Eggs	200 g
	½ oz	Vanilla	14 g
	½ oz	Baking powder	14 g
	11 oz	Pastry flour	310 g
	6 oz	Sugar	170 g
1 lb	1 oz	Whole wheat flour	480 g
	¼ oz	Cinnamon	7 g
6 lb	3 oz	Total weight	2835 g

PROCEDURE

1. Puree pinto beans with liquid.
2. Mix beans, margarine, oil, skim milk, and cocoa, and bring to a boil. Remove from heat.
3. Dissolve soda in buttermilk.
4. Add buttermilk, eggs, and vanilla to bean mixture.
5. Stir in baking powder, flours, sugar, and cinnamon.
6. Spread cake batter into lightly greased 18 × 26 in (46 × 66 cm) sheet pan.
7. Bake at 350° F (175° C) about 20 minutes or until cake springs back when lightly touched.
8. Spread glaze on warm cake, and sprinkle with walnuts.

Glaze

1 oz	Skim milk	28 g
4 oz	Confectioners' sugar	113 g
½ oz	Cocoa powder	14 g
½ tsp	Vanilla	3 g
½ oz	Margarine	14 g
3 oz	Walnuts, chopped	85 g

1. Heat milk until hot.

2. Combine milk, confectioners' sugar, cocoa, margarine, and vanilla, and beat until smooth.

LEMON CHIFFON CHEESECAKE

YIELD:	One 12 × 20 in (30 × 50 cm) pan *or* two 9 in (22 ½ cm) pies
PORTIONS:	24
PORTION SIZE:	4 oz (113 g)

Nutritional Information per Serving		
	Amount	*Calories*
Calories		165
Fat	4 g	36
Saturated fatty acid	1 g	9
Cholesterol	57 mg	
Carbohydrate	23 g	
Added sugars	16 g	
Fiber	<1 g	
Protein	9 g	
Sodium	139 mg	
Potassium	62 mg	
Vitamin A	56 RE	
Vitamin C	1 mg	
Calcium	194 mg	
Iron	<1 mg	

	1 oz	Gelatin, unflavored	28 g
	7 oz	Sugar	200 g
	2 ½ oz	Egg yolks	70 g
1 lb	1 oz	Skim milk	490 g
	¼ oz	Lemon rind, grated	7 g
3 lb	4 oz	Ricotta cheese, low-fat (1 gm fat per serving)	1480 g
	1 oz	Lemon juice, fresh	28 g
	½ oz	Vanilla	14 g
	7 oz	Egg whites, pasteurized, thawed (for fresh egg whites, see alternative method)	200 g
	7 oz	Sugar	200 g
	½ tsp	Cream of tartar	1 g
	½ oz	Vanilla	14 g
6 lb		Total weight	2730 g

PROCEDURE

1. Combine gelatin and sugar in a pan over boiling water bath.
2. Beat together egg yolks and milk.
3. Add to gelatin mixture.
4. Cook over hot water until gelatin dissolves and mixture thickens, about 10 minutes; remove from heat.
5. Add grated lemon peel; cool.
6. Puree ricotta cheese with lemon juice and vanilla. Stir into gelatin mixture.
7. Chill mixture, stirring occasionally until mixture mounds slightly when dropped from spoon.
8. Whip egg whites, sugar, and cream of tartar until stiff.
9. Stir in vanilla.
10. Fold egg white mixture into cooled gelatin mixture, mixing until smooth.
11. Pour into pan (or pans) prepared with crumb crust.

12. Sprinkle reserved crumbs over the top.

13. Chill about 4 hours. Keep chilled until ready to serve.

ALTERNATIVE METHOD (FOR FRESH EGG WHITES)

8. Whip egg whites, sugar, cream of tartar, and 5 oz (140 g) water over a boiling water bath until egg whites are stiff and temperature reaches 150° F (65° C).

Note: (1) Use same amounts of ingredients as specified for frozen pasteurized egg whites. (2) Do not let the temperature of mixture exceed 150° F (65° C)

Crust and Topping

½ oz	Margarine, softened	14 g
4½ oz	Graham cracker crumbs	120 g
½ tsp	Cinnamon	1 g
1 tsp	Nutmeg	2 g

1. Combine cracker crumbs, sugar, and spices. Cut in margarine. Reserve ½ oz (14 g) crumbs for topping.

2. Firmly press crumb mixture into a 12 × 20 in (30 × 50 cm) shallow steam table pan or two 9 in (22½ cm) pie pans.

PEANUT SQUARES

YIELD: 1 sheet pan, 18 × 26 in (46 × 66 cm)
PORTIONS: 52
PORTION SIZE: 2 oz (57 g)

Nutritional Information per Serving		
	Amount	*Calories*
Calories		166
Fat	7 g	63
Saturated fatty acid	1 g	9
Cholesterol	31 mg	
Carbohydrate	23 g	
Added sugars	15 g	
Fiber	1 g	
Protein	4 g	
Sodium	86 mg	
Potassium	102 mg	
Vitamin A	21 RE	
Vitamin C	0 mg	
Calcium	25 mg	
Iron	1 mg	

	15 oz	Pastry flour	425 g
	1 oz	Baking powder	28 g
	10½ oz	Eggs	300 g
	4½ oz	Egg whites	130 g
	14 oz	Sugar	400 g
1 lb		Water, boiling	450 g
	1 oz	Vanilla	28 g
3 lb	14 oz	Total weight	1760 g

PROCEDURE

1. Sift together flour and baking powder.
2. Beat eggs until thick and lemon-colored, about 3 minutes on high speed of mixer. Gradually add sugar, beating constantly at medium speed 4 to 5 minutes.
3. Quickly add sifted dry ingredients to egg mixture; stir just until blended.
4. Stir in hot water and vanilla.
5. Pour into lightly greased 18 × 26 in (46 × 66 cm) sheet pan.
6. Bake at 350° F (175° C) about 20 to 25 minutes or until lightly browned. Cool cake in pan 15 minutes. Cut 13 x 4 (52 pieces) and glaze.

Glaze

	2 oz	Margarine, soft-spread, low-fat	56 g
	13 oz	Confectioners' sugar	380 g
	4 oz	Skim milk	120 g
1 lb	8 oz	Peanut granules or finely ground peanuts	680 g

1. Combine margarine, sugar, and milk in bowl, and beat until smooth.
2. Dip each square into glaze so that sides and top are covered.
3. Dip immediately into peanut granules.

CARROT CAKE WITH CREAMY FROSTING

YIELD: 1 sheet pan, 18 × 26 in (46 × 66 cm)
PORTIONS: 32
PORTION SIZE: 3 ⅗ oz (102 g)

Nutritional Information per Serving		
	Amount	Calories
Calories		185
Fat	6 g	54
Saturated fatty acid	2 g	18
Cholesterol	25 mg	
Carbohydrate	31 g	
Added sugars	14 g	
Fiber	2 g	
Protein	4 g	
Sodium	268 mg	
Potassium	187 mg	
Vitamin A	514 RE	
Vitamin C	3 mg	
Calcium	41 mg	
Iron	1 mg	

	14 oz	Pastry flour	400 g
	6 oz	Whole wheat flour	170 g
	1 oz	Baking soda	28 g
	¼ oz	Cinnamon	7 g
	1 ½ tsp	Allspice	3 g
	½ tsp	Nutmeg	1 g
	12 oz	Brown sugar	340 g
	3 oz	Oil	85 g
	4 oz	Eggs	113 g
	5 oz	Egg whites	140 g
1 lb	6 oz	Carrots, shredded	625 g
	5 oz	Raisins	165 g
	11 oz	Buttermilk	320 g
1 lb		Pineapple, crushed, in unsweetened juice	454 g
6 lb	3 oz	Total weight	2850 g

PROCEDURE

1. Combine the first six ingredients.

2. Combine sugar and oil; mix for 1 minute on second speed.

3. Add eggs and egg whites; mix well.

4. Stir in carrots, raisins, buttermilk, and pineapple.

5. Add flour mixture; mix well.

6. Pour batter into lightly greased 18 × 26 in (46 × 66 cm) sheet pan.

7. Bake at 350° F (175° C) about 35 minutes or until a wooden pick comes out clean. Cool completely and frost.

Creamy Frosting

12 oz	Neufchatel cheese	340 g
5 oz	Confectioners' sugar	140 g
1 oz	Lemon juice, fresh	30 g
1 tsp	Vanilla extract	3 g
¼ oz	Lemon rind, grated	7 g

Combine all ingredients and beat 2 minutes or until creamy.

11   PIES AND PASTRIES

The pie is a truly American dessert. Perhaps that's why it's such a popular one. However, with lard or shortening as the main ingredient in their crusts, pies may seem out of place in a text about healthful baking. We've used modified crumb crusts or toppings, or simply rolled a regular crust thinner. You'll find the tradition of old-fashioned pies still preserved in recipes for pumpkin, apple, and cherry pies.

FORMULAS

Orange Chiffon Pie
Chocolate Chiffon Pie
Vanilla (or Chocolate) Cream
    Pie
Pumpkin Pie
Raspberry (or Strawberry)
    Cream Pie
Crumb-Topped Apple Pie
Mint-Chocolate Freezer Pie
Tin Roof Freezer Pie

Cherry Freezer Pie
Raspberry (or Strawberry)
    Yogurt Pie
Strawberry Tartlets
Fresh Fruit Tart
Banana-Orange Tart
Pear-Almond Tart
Eclairs
Cherry Turnovers
Prune Pockets

ORANGE CHIFFON PIE

YIELD: Four 9 in (23 cm) pies
PORTIONS: 32 (8 servings per pie)
PORTION SIZE: 3¾ oz (105 g)

Nutritional Information per Serving		
	Amount	*Calories*
Calories		150
Fat	4 g	36
Saturated fatty acid	1 g	9
Cholesterol	1 mg	
Carbohydrate	23 g	
Added sugars	7 g	
Fiber	1 g	
Protein	4 g	
Sodium	83 mg	
Potassium	121 mg	
Vitamin A	57 RE	
Vitamin C	20 mg	
Calcium	71 mg	
Iron	1 mg	

Crust

	12 oz	Cake flour	340 g
	6 oz	Margarine	170 g
	6 oz	Ice water	170 g

Filling

	1 oz	Unflavored gelatin	28 g
1 lb	8 oz	Water, cold	680 g
1 lb		Orange juice concentrate, thawed	450 g
2 lb	8 oz	Yogurt, nonfat, plain	1130 g
	8oz	Egg whites, pasteurized, room temperature	230 g
	1 tsp	Cream of tartar	1 g
	8 oz	Sugar	230 g
6 lb	1 oz	Total weight of filling	2749 g

PROCEDURE

CRUST

1. Cut margarine into flour until mixture resembles coarse meal.

2. Sprinkle ice water over mixture, and mix just until dough forms a ball. (The entire amount of water may not be needed.) Chill dough, if necessary, until it is firm enough to be easily rolled out.

3. Scale dough into four 6 oz (170 g) pieces.

4. Roll out each piece to fit four 9 in (23 cm) pie pans. Prick crusts with a fork.

5. Prebake crusts at 400° F (200° C) for 8 to 10 minutes or until light brown.

FILLING

1. Soften gelatin in cold water for 5 minutes. Dissolve over low heat.
2. Stir in orange juice concentrate and yogurt.
3. Chill until mixture mounds on a spoon.
4. Whip egg whites with cream of tartar to form soft peaks.
5. Slowly add sugar while whipping to firm peaks.
6. Gently fold whites into yogurt-orange mixture.
7. Scale 24 oz (680 g) filling into each prepared pie crust. Garnish, if desired, with orange slices. Chill until set, about 3 hours. Keep refrigerated.

CHOCOLATE CHIFFON PIE

YIELD:	Four 9 in (23 cm) pies
PORTIONS:	32 (8 servings per pie)
PORTION SIZE:	3¾ oz (105 g) slice

Nutritional Information per Serving		
	Amount	*Calories*
Calories		194
Fat	5 g	45
Saturated fatty acid	1 g	9
Cholesterol	2 mg	
Carbohydrate	33 g	
Added sugars	16 g	
Fiber	1 g	
Protein	6 g	
Sodium	113 mg	
Potassium	210 mg	
Vitamin A	103 RE	
Vitamin C	<1 mg	
Calcium	133 mg	
Iron	1 mg	

Crust

12 oz	Cake flour	340 g
6 oz	Margarine	170 g
6 oz	Ice water	170 g

Filling

	1½ oz	Unflavored gelatin	43 g
1 lb		Water, cold	450 g
	8 oz	Sugar	230 g
	4 oz	Cocoa	110 g
2 lb		Skim milk, evaporated	900 g
	1 oz	Vanilla	28 g
	8 oz	Egg whites, pasteurized, thawed	220 g
	1 tsp	Cream of tartar	2 g
	12 oz	Sugar	340 g
1 lb		Skim milk, evaporated, placed in freezer until milk freezes around edges	450 g
6 lb	2 oz	Total weight of filling	2773 g

PROCEDURE

CRUST

1. Cut margarine into flour until mixture resembles coarse meal.

2. Sprinkle ice water over mixture, and mix just until dough forms a ball. (The entire amount of water may not be needed.) Chill dough, if necessary, until it is firm enough to be easily rolled out.

3. Scale dough into four 6 oz (170 g) pieces.

4. Roll out each piece to fit four 9 in (23 cm) pie pans. Prick crusts with a fork.

5. Prebake crusts at 400° F (200° C) for 8 to 10 minutes or until light brown.

FILLING

1. Soften gelatin in cold water for 5 minutes.
2. Bring 2 lb (900 g) evaporated skim milk, sugar, and cocoa to a boil.
3. Stir into gelatin and cook over low heat until gelatin is dissolved.
4. Remove from heat and add vanilla.
5. Chill until mixture mounds on a spoon.
6. Whip egg whites with cream of tartar to form soft peaks.
7. Gradually add sugar while whipping to firm peaks.
8. Whip 1 lb (450 g) iced evaporated skim milk to peaks.
9. Fold egg whites into chilled chocolate mixture.
10. Fold in whipped milk.
11. Scale 24 oz (680 g) filling into each prepared pie crust. Chill until set, about 3 hours. Keep refrigerated.

VANILLA (OR CHOCOLATE) CREAM PIE

YIELD: Four 9 in (23 cm) pies
PORTIONS: 32 (8 servings per pie)
PORTION SIZE: 4 ¼ oz (120 g) slice

Crust

12 oz	Cake flour	340 g
6 oz	Margarine	170 g
6 oz	Ice water	170 g

Filling

	12 oz	Sugar	340 g
	6 oz	Cornstarch*	170 g
	6 oz	Nonfat dry milk	170 g
5 lb		Skim milk	2250 g
	6 oz	Egg yolks	170 g
	2 oz	Vanilla	55 g
7 lb		Total weight of filling	3155 g

PROCEDURE

CRUST

1. Cut margarine into flour until mixture resembles coarse meal.
2. Sprinkle ice water over mixture, and mix just until dough forms a ball. (The entire amount of water may not be needed.) Chill dough, if necessary, until it is firm enough to be easily rolled out.
3. Scale dough into four 6 oz (170 g) pieces.
4. Roll out each piece to fit four 9 in (23 cm) pie pans. Prick crusts with a fork.
5. Prebake crusts at 400° F (200° C) for 8 to 10 minutes or until light brown.

FILLING

1. Combine sugar, cornstarch, and nonfat milk solids. Stir into skim milk.
2. Cook mixture until thickened.
3. Stir in egg yolks. Return to heat and cook 1 minute longer.
4. Remove from heat and add vanilla.
5. Scale 28 oz (790 g) filling into each prepared pie crust. Keep refrigerated.

* For Chocolate Cream Pie, add 4 oz (110 g) cocoa with the cornstarch.

Nutritional Information per Serving (Vanilla Cream Pie)

	Amount	Calories
Calories		194
Fat	6 g	54
Saturated fatty acid	1 g	9
Cholesterol	70 mg	
Carbohydrate	29 g	
Added sugars	11 g	
Fiber	<1 g	
Protein	6 g	
Sodium	119 mg	
Potassium	227 mg	
Vitamin A	165 RE	
Vitamin C	1 mg	
Calcium	164 mg	
Iron	1 mg	

Nutritional Information per Serving (Chocolate Cream Pie)

	Amount	Calories
Calories		203
Fat	7 g	63
Saturated fatty acid	2 g	18
Cholesterol	70 mg	
Carbohydrate	30 g	
Added sugars	11 g	
Fiber	1 g	
Protein	7 g	
Sodium	120 mg	
Potassium	268 mg	
Vitamin A	165 RE	
Vitamin C	1 mg	
Calcium	169 mg	
Iron	1 mg	

PUMPKIN PIE

YIELD:	Four 9 in (23 cm) pies
PORTIONS:	32 (8 servings per pie)
PORTION SIZE:	4 oz (113 g)

Nutritional Information per Serving		
	Amount	*Calories*
Calories		162
Fat	5 g	45
Saturated fatty acid	2 g	18
Cholesterol	1 mg	
Carbohydrate	25 g	
Added sugars	12 g	
Fiber	1 g	
Protein	4 g	
Sodium	96 mg	
Potassium	230 mg	
Vitamin A	955 RE	
Vitamin C	7 g	
Calcium	96 mg	
Iron	1 mg	

Crust

7¾ oz		Pastry flour	220 g
5 oz		Shortening, vegetable	140 g
½ tsp		Salt	3 g
4 to 5 oz		Ice water	114 to 130 g

Filling

2 lb	11 oz	Pumpkin, canned	1230 g
1 lb	8 oz	Skim milk, evaporated	680 g
	11 oz	Orange juice, reconstituted	320 g
	11 oz	Dark corn syrup	320 g
	4 oz	Brown sugar	55 g
	¼ oz	Cinnamon	6 g
	2 tsp	Allspice	4 g
	¾ tsp	Ginger	1½ g
	¾ tsp	Cloves	1½ g
	14 oz	Egg whites	400 g
6 lb	11 oz	Total weight of filling	3018 g

PROCEDURE

CRUST

1. Combine flour and salt. Cut in shortening until mixture resembles coarse meal.

2. Sprinkle ice water over mixture, and mix just until mixture forms a ball. (The entire amount of water may not be needed.)

3. Scale dough into four 4 oz (113 g) pieces. (Refrigerate pieces until you are ready to work with them.)

4. Roll out each piece to fit a 9 in (23 cm) pieplate.

5. Trim excess dough; fold edges under and flute.

FILLING

1. Combine all filling ingredients and beat until well-blended.

2. Divide pumpkin mixture evenly among pie shells, using about 25 oz (715 g) per shell.

3. Bake at 350° F (175° C) for about one hour or until a knife inserted into center comes out clean.

RASPBERRY (OR STRAWBERRY) CREAM PIE

YIELD: Three 9 in (23 cm) pies
PORTIONS: 24
PORTION SIZE: 5 oz (142 g)

Nutritional Information per Serving		
	Amount	*Calories*
Calories		174
Fat	5 g	45
Saturated fatty acid	1 g	9
Cholesterol	<1 mg	
Carbohydrate	31 g	
Added sugars	13 g	
Fiber	3 g	
Protein	3 g	
Sodium	70 mg	
Potassium	139 mg	
Vitamin A	27 RE	
Vitamin C	16 mg	
Calcium	56 mg	
Iron	2 mg	

Crust

	6 oz	Pastry flour	170 g
	½ tsp	Salt	3 g
	4 oz	Shortening, vegetable	113 g
	2 to 3 oz	Ice water	56 to 86 g

Filling

1 lb	10 oz	Skim milk	710 g
	5 oz	Sugar	140 g
	1 oz	Cornstarch	21 g
	5 oz	Egg whites	140 g
1 lb	2 oz	Raspberry (or strawberry) juice	510 g
	6 oz	Sugar	170 g
	1½ oz	Cornstarch	43 g
	¾ oz	Lemon juice, fresh	21 g
2 lb	8 oz	Raspberries (or strawberries)	1135 g
6 lb	7 oz	Total weight of filling	2925 g

PROCEDURE

1. Combine flour and salt. Cut in shortening until mixture resembles coarse meal.

2. Sprinkle ice water over mixture, and mix just until mixture forms a ball. (The entire amount of water may not be needed.) Chill dough, if necessary, until it is firm enough to be easily rolled out.

3. Scale dough into three 4⅓ oz (123 g) pieces.

4. Roll out each piece to fit a 9 in (23 cm) pie pan. Flute edges, if desired.

5. Prick shells with a fork and bake at 400° F (200° C) until light brown.

FILLING

1. Mix together milk, sugar, cornstarch, and egg whites in a large saucepan. Boil until thick, stirring constantly, about 15 minutes.

2. Scale 12 oz (340 g) custard into each pie shell. Set aside.

3. In a large saucepan, mix juice, cornstarch, lemon juice, and sugar. Boil until thick and clear, stirring constantly.

4. Cool and add berries.

5. Scale 22 oz (625 g) berry filling into each shell and spread over custard filling. Keep refrigerated.

CRUMB-TOPPED APPLE PIE

YIELD:	Four 9 in (23 cm) pies
PORTIONS:	32 (8 servings per pie)
PORTION SIZE:	4 oz (110 g) slice

Nutritional Information per Serving		
	Amount	Calories
Calories		231
Fat	7 g	63
Saturated fatty acid	1 g	9
Cholesterol	0 mg	
Carbohydrate	40 g	
Added sugars	11 g	
Fiber	3 g	
Protein	3 g	
Sodium	79 mg	
Potassium	142 mg	
Vitamin A	82 RE	
Vitamin C	2 mg	
Calcium	15 mg	
Iron	2 mg	

Crust

12 oz	Cake Flour	340 g
6 oz	Margarine	170 g
6 oz	Ice water	170 g

Filling

4 lb		Fresh apples, peeled, cored, sliced	1800 g
	8 oz	Apple juice concentrate, thawed	230 g
	4 oz	Cornstarch	110 g
	2 tsp	Cinnamon	9 g
	1 tsp	Nutmeg	4 g
4 lb	12 oz	Total weight of filling	2153 g

PROCEDURE

CRUST

1. Cut margarine into flour until mixture resembles coarse meal.
2. Sprinkle ice water over mixture, and mix just until dough forms a ball. (The entire 6 oz of water may not be necessary.) Chill dough, if necessary, until it is stiff enough to be easily rolled out.
3. Scale dough into four 6 oz (170 g) pieces.
4. Roll out each piece to fit four 9 in (23 cm) pie pans. Set aside.

FILLING

1. Toss apple slices with apple juice concentrate.
2. Combine cornstarch, cinnamon, and nutmeg. Stir into apple slices.
3. Place 1 lb 3 oz (540 g) apple filling into each pie shell.
4. Sprinkle 6 oz (170 g) crumb topping over apples.
5. Bake at 400° F (200° C) for 35 to 40 minutes or until apples are tender.

Crumb Topping

10 oz	Sugar	280 g
6 oz	Pastry flour	170 g
8 oz	Oats, quick	230 g
3 oz	Margarine	85 g
1 lb 11 oz	Total weight of topping	765 g

Combine sugar, flour, and oats. Cut in margarine.

MINT CHOCOLATE FREEZER PIE

YIELD:	Four 9 in (23 cm) pies	
PORTIONS:	32 (8 servings per pie)	
PORTION SIZE:	3½ oz (100 g) slice	

Nutritional Information per Serving		
	Amount	Calories
Calories		181
Fat	6 g	54
Saturated fatty acid	3 g	27
Cholesterol	8 mg	
Carbohydrate	30 g	
Added sugars	NA*	
Fiber	2 g	
Protein	4 g	
Sodium	130 mg	
Potassium	232 mg	
Vitamin A	41 RE	
Vitamin C	2 mg	
Calcium	92 mg	
Iron	1 mg	
* NA = not available		

Crust

	12 oz	Graham cracker crumbs	340 g
	4 oz	Cocoa	110 g
	2 oz	Margarine, melted	55 g
	4 oz	Orange juice	110 g
1 lb	6 oz	Total weight	615 g

Chocolate Sauce

	6 oz	Sugar	170 g
	4 oz	Cocoa	170 g
	1 oz	Cornstarch	28 g
1 lb		Water	450 g
	1 oz	Vanilla	28 g
1 lb	12 oz	Total weight	786 g

Filling

4 lb		Vanilla ice milk, softened	1800 g
	1 tsp	Peppermint extract	5 g
4 lb		Total weight	1805 g

PROCEDURE

CRUST

1. Combine crust ingredients.

2. Scale 5½ oz (155 g) crumbs into four 9 in (23 cm) pie tins. Press crumbs firmly against bottom and sides to form crust.

3. Bake crusts at 375° F (190° C) for 5 to 7 minutes or until slightly browned. Cool before filling.

FILLING

1. Combine softened ice milk and peppermint extract.
2. Pour 3 oz (85 g) chocolate sauce into each prepared pie shell. Spread carefully over bottoms.
3. Scale 1 lb (450 g) minted ice milk over sauce, smoothing top.
4. Freeze until firm. Remove from freezer.
5. Spread 4 oz (110 g) chocolate sauce carefully over ice milk. Freeze until firm. Remove from freezer 10 minutes before serving.

CHOCOLATE SAUCE

1. Combine all ingredients except vanilla. Cook over medium heat until thickened, stirring often.
2. Remove from heat. Stir in vanilla.

TIN ROOF FREEZER PIE

YIELD:		Four 9 in (23 cm) pies	
PORTIONS:		32 (8 servings per pie)	
PORTION SIZE:		3½ oz (100 g) slice	

Nutritional Information per Serving		
	Amount	*Calories*
Calories		202
Fat	7 g	63
Saturated fatty acid	3 g	27
Cholesterol	8 mg	
Carbohydrate	32 g	
Added sugars	NA*	
Fiber	2 g	
Protein	5 g	
Sodium	151 mg	
Potassium	219 mg	
Vitamin A	41 RE	
Vitamin C	2 mg	
Calcium	91 mg	
Iron	1 mg	
* NA = not available.		

Crust

1 lb		Graham cracker crumbs	450 g
	2 oz	Margarine, melted	55 g
	4 oz	Orange juice	110 g
1 lb	6 oz	Total weight	615 g

Chocolate Sauce

	6 oz	Sugar	170 g
	4 oz	Cocoa	110 g
	1 oz	Cornstarch	28 g
1 lb		Water	450 g
	1 oz	Vanilla	28 g
1 lb	12 oz	Total weight	786 g

Filling

4 lb		Vanilla ice milk, softened	1800 g
	3 oz	Peanuts, unsalted	85 g
4 lb	3 oz	Total weight	1885 g

PROCEDURE

CRUST

1. Combine crust ingredients.

2. Scale 5½ oz (155 g) crumbs into four 9 in (23 cm) pie tins. Press crumbs firmly against bottom and sides to form crust.

3. Bake crusts at 375° F (190° C) for 5 to 7 minutes or until slightly browned. Cool before filling.

FILLING

1. Combine softened ice milk and peanuts.

2. Swirl chocolate sauce into ice milk.

3. Scale 1 lb 7 oz (650 g) ice milk mixture into each prepared pie shell.

4. Freeze until firm. Remove from freezer 10 minutes before serving.

CHOCOLATE SAUCE

1. Combine all ingredients except vanilla. Cook until thickened, stirring often.

2. Remove from heat. Stir in vanilla.

CHERRY FREEZER PIE

YIELD:	Four 9 in (23 cm) pies
PORTIONS:	32 (8 servings per pie)
PORTION SIZE:	3½ oz (100 g) slice

	Nutritional Information per Serving	
	Amount	*Calories*
Calories		181
Fat	6 g	54
Saturated fatty acid	3 g	27
Cholesterol	10 mg	
Carbohydrate	29 g	
Added sugars	NA*	
Fiber	1 g	
Protein	4 g	
Sodium	161 mg	
Potassium	205 mg	
Vitamin A	58 RE	
Vitamin C	2 mg	
Calcium	104 mg	
Iron	1 mg	
* NA = not available.		

Crust

1 lb		Graham cracker crumbs	450 g
	2 oz	Margarine, melted	55 g
	4 oz	Orange juice	110 g
1 lb	6 oz	Total weight	615 g

Filling

5 lb		Vanilla ice milk, softened	2260 g
1 lb		Sour cherries, chopped	450 g
	1 tsp	Almond extract	5 g
6 lb		Total weight	2715 g

PROCEDURE

CRUST

1. Combine crust ingredients.
2. Scale 5½ oz (155 g) crumbs into four 9 in (23 cm) pie tins. Press crumbs firmly against bottom and sides to form crust.
3. Prebake crusts at 375° F (190° C) for 5 to 7 minutes or until slightly browned. Cool before filling.

FILLING

1. Combine softened ice milk, cherries, and almond extract.
2. Scale 1 lb 8 oz (680 g) ice milk mixture into each prepared pie shell.
3. Freeze until firm. Remove from freezer 10 minutes before serving.

RASPBERRY (OR STRAWBERRY) YOGURT PIE

YIELD: Four 9 in (23 cm) pies
PORTIONS: 32 (8 servings per pie)
PORTION SIZE: 4½ oz (125 g) slice

Nutritional Information per Serving		
	Amount	*Calories*
Calories		190
Fat	7 g	63
Saturated fatty acid	3 g	27
Cholesterol	12 g	
Carbohydrate	27 g	
Added sugars	11 g	
Fiber	1 g	
Protein	6 g	
Sodium	196 mg	
Potassium	125 mg	
Vitamin A	75 RE	
Vitamin C	22 mg	
Calcium	91 mg	
Iron	1 mg	

Crust

1 lb		Graham cracker crumbs	450 g
	2 oz	Margarine, melted	55 g
	4 oz	Orange juice	110 g
1 lb	6 oz	Total weight	615 g

Filling

	4 oz	Water	110 g
	½ oz	Gelatin, unflavored	14 g
2 lb		Yogurt, nonfat, plain	900 g
1 lb		Neufchatel cheese, softened	450 g
1 lb		Low-fat sour cream, (2 g fat per oz)	450 g
	12 oz	Honey	340 g
	½ oz	Vanilla	14 g
2 lb	8 oz	Raspberries (or strawberries), fresh	1100 g
7 lb	9 oz	Total weight	3378 g

PROCEDURE

CRUST

1. Combine crust ingredients.
2. Scale 5½ oz (155 g) crumbs into four 9 in (23 cm) pie tins. Press crumbs firmly against bottom and sides to form crusts.
3. Prebake crusts at 375° F (190° C) for 5 to 7 minutes or until slightly browned. Cool before filling.

FILLING

1. Soften gelatin in water for 5 minutes. Cook over low heat until gelatin is dissolved.
2. Combine remaining ingredients except raspberries and beat until smooth.
3. Stir in dissolved gelatin.
4. Scale 1 lb 4 oz (560 g) yogurt mixture into each prepared pie shell.
5. Freeze until firm. Remove from freezer 10 minutes before serving.
6. Top each pie with 10 oz (280 g) fresh raspberries.

STRAWBERRY TARTLETS

YIELD:	2⅔ dozen
PORTIONS:	32
PORTION SIZE:	2¾ oz (80 g)

Crust

	12 oz	Cake flour	340 g
	6 oz	Margarine	170 g
	6 oz	Ice water	170 g
1 lb	8 oz	Total weight	680 g
	2 oz	Apricot jam, sugar-free	55 g

Filling

2 lb		Strawberries,* fresh	900 g
	3 oz	Sugar	85 g
	1¼ oz	Cornstarch	35 g
	2 oz	Water	55 g
2 lb		Fresh strawberries	900 g
4 lb	8 oz	Total weight	2030 g

* If using frozen strawberries, thaw and then mash. Drain off 4 oz (110 g) juice and combine with cornstarch. Bring strawberries and sugar to a boil. Stir in cornstarch mixture and cook until thickened. Cool.

PROCEDURE

CRUST

1. Cut margarine into flour until mixture resembles coarse meal.

2. Sprinkle ice water over mixture, and mix just until dough forms a ball. (The entire 6 oz of water may not be needed.) Chill dough, if necessary, until it is firm enough to be easily rolled out.

3. Roll out dough ¼ in (½ cm) thick.

4. Cut dough circles to fit tartlet pans, 1 in (2½ cm) depth, 3 in (7½ cm) top diameter, and 1¾ in (4½ cm) bottom diameter; approximately ¾ oz (21 g) dough per circle. Fit circles into lightly greased tartlet pans.

5. Bake crusts at 400° F (200° C) for 7 to 10 minutes or until golden brown. Brush inside of tart shells with half of apricot glaze.

Nutritional Information per Serving		
	Amount	*Calories*
Calories		108
Fat	4 g	36
Saturated fatty acid	1 g	9
Cholesterol	0 mg	
Carbohydrate	16 g	
Added sugars	3 g	
Fiber	2 g	
Protein	1 g	
Sodium	52 mg	
Potassium	102 mg	
Vitamin A	55 RE	
Vitamin C	28 mg	
Calcium	12 mg	
Iron	1 mg	

FILLING

1. Mash strawberries, but do not puree. Stir in sugar.
2. Bring to a boil over medium heat.
3. Dissolve cornstarch in water.
4. Add to strawberries and cook until thickened. Cool before using.
5. Scale 1 oz (28 g) filling into each tartlet shell.
6. Garnish each with a fresh strawberry.
7. Brush tarts with other half of apricot glaze. Keep refrigerated.

APRICOT GLAZE

Heat apricot jam to a boil. Remove from heat and strain. Use while hot.

FRESH FRUIT TART

YIELD:	Four 10 in (25 cm) tarts
PORTIONS:	32 (8 servings per tart)
PORTION SIZE:	4 ¼ oz (120 g) slice

Crust

12 oz	Cake flour	340 g
6 oz	Margarine	170 g
6 oz	Ice water	170 g

Filling

2 lb 2 oz	Low-fat ricotta cheese (1 g fat per oz)	950 g
4 oz	Sugar	110 g
2 oz	Lemon juice	55 g
¼ oz	Grated lemon rind	7 g
¼ oz	Vanilla	7 g
4 lb	Assorted fresh fruit	1800 g
8 oz	Apricot jam, sugar-free	230 g
7 lb	Total weight of filling	3159 g

PROCEDURE

CRUST

1. Cut margarine into flour until mixture resembles coarse meal.
2. Sprinkle ice water over mixture, and mix just until dough forms a ball. (The entire amount of water may not be needed.) Chill dough, if necessary, until it is firm enough to be easily rolled out.
3. Scale dough into four 6 oz (170 g) pieces.
4. Roll out each piece to fit four 10 in (25 cm) tart pans with removable bottoms.
5. Bake crusts at 400° F (200° C) for 8 to 10 minutes or until crisp.

FILLING

1. Combine all filling ingredients except fruit and apricot glaze and whip until smooth.
2. Scale 10 oz (280 g) filling into each prepared tart crust. Spread evenly.
3. Top each with 1 lb (450 g) of assorted fresh fruit.
4. Brush fruit with hot apricot glaze. Keep refrigerated.

APRICOT GLAZE

Heat apricot jam to a boil. Remove from heat and strain. Use while hot.

Nutritional Information per Serving		
	Amount	Calories
Calories		152
Fat	6 g	54
Saturated fatty acid	1 g	9
Cholesterol	4 mg	
Carbohydrate	23 g	
Added sugars	4 g	
Fiber	2 g	
Protein	5 g	
Sodium	72 mg	
Potassium	169 mg	
Vitamin A	87 RE	
Vitamin C	41 mg	
Calcium	48 mg	
Iron	1 mg	

BANANA-ORANGE TART

YIELD: Four 10 in (25 cm) tarts
PORTIONS: 40 (10 servings per tart)
PORTION SIZE: 4 oz (110 g) slice

Crust

	12 oz	Cake flour	340 g
	6 oz	Margarine	170 g
	6 oz	Ice water	170 g

Filling

1 lb		Bananas	450 g
1 lb	8 oz	Apricot jam, sugar-free	680 g
3 lb		Bananas, peeled and sliced	1350 g
2 lb		Mandarin oranges, canned, packed in light syrup, drained	900 g
	12 oz	Apricot jam, sugar-free	340 g
8 lb	4 oz	Total weight of filling	3720 g

Nutritional Information per Serving

	Amount	Calories
Calories		175
Fat	4 g	36
Saturated fatty acid	<1 g	6
Cholesterol	0 mg	
Carbohydrate	39 g	
Added sugars	0 g	
Fiber	2 g	
Protein	1 g	
Sodium	45 mg	
Potassium	231 mg	
Vitamin A	56 RE	
Vitamin C	9 mg	
Calcium	12 mg	
Iron	1 mg	

PROCEDURE

CRUST

1. Cut margarine into flour until mixture resembles coarse meal.
2. Sprinkle ice water over mixture, and mix just until dough forms a ball. (The entire 6 oz of water may not be needed.) Chill dough, if necessary, until it is firm enough to be easily rolled out.
3. Scale dough into four 6 oz (170 g) pieces.
4. Roll out each piece to fit four 10 in (25 cm) tart pans with removable bottoms.
5. Bake crusts at 400° F (200° C) for 8 to 10 minutes or until crisp.

FILLING

1. Puree 1 lb (450 g) bananas with the 1 lb 8 oz (680 g) apricot jam until smooth.
2. Spread 10 oz (280 g) puree in bottom of each prepared tart shell.
3. Arrange 12 oz (340 g) banana slices and 8 oz (220 g) mandarin oranges over filling.
4. Brush fruit with hot apricot glaze. Keep refrigerated. Serve the same day.

APRICOT GLAZE

Heat 12 oz (340 g) apricot jam to a boil. Remove from heat and strain. Use while hot.

PEAR-ALMOND TART

YIELD: One 12 × 20 in (30 × 50 cm)
PORTIONS: 35
PORTION SIZE: 4 oz (113 g)

Nutritional Information per Serving		
	Amount	*Calories*
Calories		115
Fat	4 g	36
Saturated fatty acid	<1 g	
Cholesterol	0 mg	
Carbohydrate	21 g	
Added sugars	<1 g	
Fiber	3 g	
Protein	1 g	
Sodium	17 mg	
Potassium	124 mg	
Vitamin A	18 RE	
Vitamin C	4 mg	
Calcium	18 mg	
Iron	1 mg	

Filling

6 lb		Pears, fresh, peeled, sliced	2722 g
	1¾ oz	Lemon juice, fresh	50 g
1 lb	10 oz	Pear nectar	750 g
	¾ tsp	Cinnamon	3 g
	¾ tsp	Nutmeg	2 g
	1 tsp	Almond extract	4 g
7 lb	12 oz	Total weight of filling	3530 g

Crust

	2½ oz	Almonds, ground	65 g
	1 oz	Sugar	28 g
	8 oz	Pastry flour	230 g
	¼ tsp	Cinnamon	1 g
	2 oz	Margarine	55 g
	1 oz	Shortening, vegetable	25 g
	4 oz	Ice water	113 g

PROCEDURE

FILLING

1. Combine pear slices, lemon juice, nectar, spices, and almond extract.
2. Spoon mixture into a 12 × 12 in (30 × 50 cm) shallow steam table pan.

CRUST

1. Combine ground almonds, sugar, flour, and cinnamon. Cut in margarine and shortening until mixture resembles coarse meal.
2. Sprinkle ice water over mixture, and mix just until dough forms a ball. (The entire amount of water may not be needed.) Chill dough, if necessary, until it is firm enough to be easily rolled out.
3. Roll dough into a 12 × 20 in (30 × 50 cm) rectangle.
4. Place dough on top of pear mixture, cut slits to allow steam to escape.
5. Bake at 400 F° (200° C) about 50 minutes or until crust is lightly browned.

ECLAIRS

YIELD:	3⅔ dozen
PORTIONS:	44
PORTION SIZE:	3 ¼ oz (90 g) serving

Nutritional Information per Serving		
	Amount	*Calories*
Calories		158
Fat	6 g	54
Saturated fatty acid	1 g	9
Cholesterol	50 mg	
Carbohydrate	22 g	
Added sugars	9 g	
Fiber	1 g	
Protein	6 g	
Sodium	105 mg	
Potassium	127 mg	
Vitamin A	98 RE	
Vitamin C	<1 mg	
Calcium	72 mg	
Iron	1 mg	

Eclair Paste

2 lb		Water	900 g
	8 oz	Margarine	230 g
1 lb	2 oz	Bread flour	500 g
	14 oz	Eggs	400 g
1 lb		Egg whites	450 g
5 lb	8 oz	Total weight	2480 g

Cream Filling

	6 oz	Sugar	170 g
	2 oz	Cornstarch	55 g
2 lb		Skim milk, evaporated	900 g
	4 oz	Eggs, beaten	110 g
	¼ oz	Vanilla	7 g
2 lb	12 oz	Total weight	1242 g

Chocolate Icing

	6 oz	Confectioners' sugar	170 g
	2 oz	Cocoa	55 g
	2 oz	Corn syrup	55 g
	2 oz	Hot water	55 g
	1 tsp	Vanilla	5 g
	12 oz	Total weight	340 g

PROCEDURE

ECLAIR PASTE

1. Bring water and margarine to a boil. Remove from heat and stir in flour.

2. Return to heat and cook until dough pulls away from sides, stirring constantly.

3. Place dough in a mixing bowl and cool slightly.

4. Beat together eggs and egg whites.

5. Slowly add egg mixture to dough, beating well after each addition.

6. Pipe out 44 eclairs onto parchment-lined sheet pans.

7. Bake at 400° F (200° C) for 35 minutes or until crisp. Cool before filling.

8. Pipe 1 oz (28 g) pastry cream into each eclair.

9. Ice with a thin coating of chocolate icing. Keep refrigerated.

FILLING

1. Combine sugar, cornstarch, and skim milk. Cook until thickened.

2. Whip in eggs and return to heat until temperature reaches 140° F. Do not boil.

3. Remove from heat. Add vanilla. Cool before using.

CHOCOLATE ICING

Beat all ingredients until smooth. Use while warm.

∂∂∂∂∂∂∂∂∂∂∂∂∂∂∂∂∂∂∂∂∂∂∂
∂∂∂∂∂∂∂∂∂∂∂∂∂∂∂∂∂∂∂∂∂∂∂

CHERRY TURNOVERS

YIELD:	2 dozen (3 lb)
PORTIONS:	24
PORTION SIZE:	2 oz (57 g)

	10 oz	12 Phyllo dough leaves	280 g
	⅔ oz	Butter-flavored pan-release spray	19 g
Filling			
1 lb	14 oz	Cherry pie filling	850 g
	1½ oz	Lemon juice, fresh	43 g
	8 oz	Neufchatel cheese or light cream cheese	230 g
2 lb	7 oz	Total weight of filling	1120 g

PROCEDURE

1. Working with 1 phyllo sheet at a time, lightly spray with butter-flavored pan-release spray. (Spray should last less than 1 second.)
2. Cut each sheet lengthwise into four 3½ in (9 cm) wide strips.
3. Stack two strips.
4. Mix cherry pie filling with lemon juice.
5. Place strip vertically on a table. Spoon 1 tbsp pie filling mixture onto each strip, spreading it to within 1 in (2½ cm) of one end (see diagram).
6. Place 1 tsp cream cheese on top of the filling.
7. Fold the left bottom corner up over the mixture, forming a triangle.
8. Keep folding back and forth, always keeping a triangle. (Folding is similar to folding a flag.)
9. Repeat with remaining phyllo sheets.
10. Place the turnovers, seam side down, onto a lightly greased baking sheet.
11. Bake at 400° F (200° C) about 15 minutes or until lightly browned. Drizzle icing over warm turnover.

Icing

7 oz	Confectioners' sugar	200 g
2 oz	Water	56 g
½ tsp	Vanilla	1 g

Beat until smooth.

Nutritional Information per Serving

	Amount	Calories
Calories		98
Fat	3 g	27
Saturated fatty acid	1 g	9
Cholesterol	7 mg	
Carbohydrate	16 g	
Added sugars	NA*	
Fiber	1 g	
Protein	2 g	
Sodium	98 mg	
Potassium	45 mg	
Vitamin A	25 RE	
Vitamin C	1 mg	
Calcium	13 mg	
Iron	<1 mg	

* NA = not available.

5.

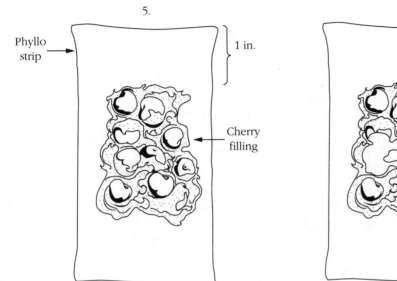

Phyllo strip

1 in.

Cherry filling

6.

Neufchatel cream cheese

7.

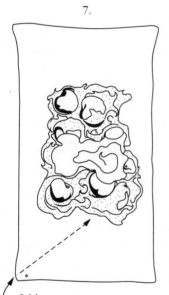

fold up

fold up

8.

fold up

PRUNE POCKETS

YIELD:	4 dozen
PORTIONS:	48
PORTION SIZE:	2 ¼ oz (64 g)

Nutritional Information per Serving		
	Amount	*Calories*
Calories		164
Fat	5 g	45
Saturated fatty acid	<1 g	2
Cholesterol	<1 mg	
Carbohydrate	28 g	
Added sugars	5 g	
Fiber	3 g	
Protein	4 g	
Sodium	92 mg	
Potassium	212 mg	
Vitamin A	32 RE	
Vitamin C	6 mg	
Calcium	35 mg	
Iron	1 mg	

Filling

1 lb	8 oz	Prunes, pitted, chopped	680 g
	4 oz	Raisins	110 g
1 lb	4 oz	Orange juice, reconstituted	560 g
	½ oz	Grated orange rind	14 g
3 lb	½ oz	Total weight of filling	1364 g

Pastry

1 lb		Cottage cheese, low-fat (1% milk fat)	450 g
	8 oz	Oil	230 g
	8 oz	Brown sugar	230 g
	4 oz	Skim milk	110 g
	½ oz	Vanilla	14 g
	12 oz	Whole wheat pastry flour	340 g
	12 oz	Pastry flour	340 g
	¾ oz	Baking powder	21 g
3 lb	13 oz	Total weight of pastry	1735 g

PROCEDURE

FILLING

1. Combine prunes, raisins, and orange juice. Cook until juice is absorbed.
2. Add orange zest. Cool filling before using.

PASTRY

1. Process cottage cheese in blender or food processor until smooth.
2. Stir in oil, sugar, skim milk, and vanilla.
3. Add flours and baking powder to cottage cheese mixture to make a stiff dough.
4. Turn out onto table surface. Knead 10 times.
5. Roll out dough to ¼ in (½ cm) thickness.
6. Cut dough into 48 squares.
7. Place 1 oz (28 g) filling in center of each pocket.
8. Fold corners of squares into middle and press. Brush with water.
9. Bake at 350° F (175° C) for 15 minutes or until pockets are golden brown.

12 DESSERTS

This chapter presents fruit desserts such as cobblers, puddings, both cooked and steamed, and a fruit mousse. These are the simple desserts that are made more elegant with sauces. Keep in mind that a sauce's purpose is to enhance a dessert, not to cover it up. We have assembled a few ideas for incorporating fiber from fruits while reducing fat and sugar content. Try experimenting with other fruits for more variety.

FORMULAS

Apple Snow with Caramel
   Sauce
Almond Cream with Choco-
   late Sauce
Peach Cobbler
Steamed Chocolate Pudding
   with Cherry Sauce

Apricot-Banana Mousse
Rice Pudding
Granny's Apple Crisp

APPLE SNOW WITH CARAMEL SAUCE

YIELD: 2 dozen
PORTIONS: 24
PORTION SIZE: 4½ oz (130 g)

Nutritional Information per Serving		
	Amount	*Calories*
Calories		156
Fat	3 g	27
Saturated fatty acid	<1 g	5
Cholesterol	0 mg	
Carbohydrate	33 g	
Added sugars	17 g	
Fiber	2 g	
Protein	1 g	
Sodium	58 mg	
Potassium	169 mg	
Vitamin A	47 RE	
Vitamin C	4 mg	
Calcium	34 mg	
Iron	<1 mg	

Apple Snow

4 lb	8 oz	Apples, peeled, cored, sliced	2050 g
	8 oz	Water	230 g
	½ oz	Vanilla	14 g
	8 oz	Sugar	230 g
	8 oz	Egg whites, pasteurized	230 g
	1 tsp	Cream of tartar	2 g
6 lb		Total weight	2756 g

Caramel Sauce

	6 oz	Brown sugar	170 g
	2 oz	Margarine, unsalted	55 g
	5 oz	Skim milk, evaporated	140 g
	½ oz	Cornstarch	14 g
	1 tsp	Vanilla	5 g
	13 oz	Total weight	384 g

PROCEDURE

APPLE SNOW

1. Cook apples and water over low heat until apples are soft.
2. Put apples through a food mill or process in a food processor until smooth.
3. Add vanilla.
4. Whip egg whites and cream of tartar to form soft peaks.
5. Gradually add sugar and whip to firm peaks.
6. Fold whites into apple mixture.
7. Spoon 4 oz (110 g) apple snow into each of 24 dessert bowls.
8. Top with ½ oz (14 g)—1 tbsp—caramel sauce. Keep refrigerated.

CARAMEL SAUCE

1. In a saucepan, melt margarine and brown sugar.
2. Dissolve cornstarch in milk.
3. Add to saucepan and bring to a boil. Boil gently two minutes, stirring constantly.
4. Remove from heat and add vanilla. Cool slightly before using.

ALMOND CREAM WITH CHOCOLATE SAUCE

YIELD:	3 dozen
PORTIONS:	36
PORTION SIZE:	4½ oz (130 g)

Almond Cream

	1½ oz	Gelatin, plain	43 g
	12 oz	Water	340 g
4 lb	10 oz	Skim milk	2100 g
1 lb		Sugar	450 g
	½ oz	Vanilla	14 g
	½ oz	Almond extract	14 g
2 lb	8 oz	Yogurt, nonfat, plain	1130 g
9 lb		Total weight	4091 g

Chocolate Sauce

	10 oz	Water	280 g
	6 oz	Sugar	170 g
	1½ oz	Cocoa	43 g
	½ oz	Cornstarch	14 g
	½ oz	Vanilla	14 g
1 lb	2 oz	Total weight	521 g

PROCEDURE

ALMOND CREAM

1. Soften gelatin in water for 5 minutes.
2. Stir in milk and sugar. Heat over low heat to dissolve gelatin and sugar.
3. Remove from heat. Stir in vanilla and almond extract.
4. Chill mixture to the consistency of unbeaten egg whites.
5. Stir in yogurt.
6. Spoon 4 oz (110 g) almond cream into each of 36 dessert bowls or parfait glasses.
7. Top with ½ oz (14 g) or 1 tbsp—chocolate sauce. Chill for several hours to set. Keep refrigerated.

CHOCOLATE SAUCE

1. In a saucepan, bring all ingredients except vanilla to a boil, stirring constantly.
2. Boil gently two minutes, stirring constantly, until slightly thickened.
3. Remove from heat and add vanilla. Cool before using.

Nutritional Information per Serving		
	Amount	Calories
Calories		112
Fat	<1 g	3
Saturated fatty acid	0 g	0
Cholesterol	2 mg	
Carbohydrate	23 g	
Added sugars	18 g	
Fiber	1 g	
Protein	5 g	
Sodium	50 mg	
Potassium	112 mg	
Vitamin A	36 RE	
Vitamin C	<1 mg	
Calcium	126 mg	
Iron	<1 mg	

PEACH COBBLER

YIELD: 1 sheet pan, 18 × 26 in (46 × 66 cm)
PORTIONS: 40
PORTION SIZE: 4 oz (113 g)

Nutritional Information per Serving		
	Amount	*Calories*
Calories		175
Fat	4 g	36
Saturated fatty acid	1 g	9
Cholesterol	<1 mg	
Carbohydrate	35 g	
Added sugars	10 g	
Fiber	1 g	
Protein	1 g	
Sodium	108 mg	
Potassium	102 mg	
Vitamin A	66 RE	
Vitamin C	56 mg	
Calcium	23 mg	
Iron	1 mg	

5 lb	4 oz	Peaches, frozen or fresh, unsweetened	2380 g
	7 oz	Sugar	210 g
	6⅓ oz	Margarine	180 g
1 lb		Pastry flour	460 g
	¾ oz	Baking powder	20 g
	9 oz	Skim milk	260 g
	1½ oz	Cornstarch	39 g
	7 oz	Sugar	210 g
2 lb	1 oz	Water, boiling	935 g
10 lb	5 oz	Total weight	4680 g

PROCEDURE

1. If using frozen peaches, thaw and drain. Wash, peel, and slice fresh peaches.

2. Spread peaches to cover the bottom of a lightly greased 18 × 26 (46 × 66 cm) sheet pan.

3. Cream first 7 oz sugar with margarine.

4. Combine flour and baking powder with milk. Add to sugar mixture.

5. Spread batter over peaches.

6. Combine remaining sugar with cornstarch. Sprinkle over top of batter.

7. Pour boiling water over all.

8. Bake at 350° F (175° C) about 1 hour or until light golden brown.

STEAMED CHOCOLATE PUDDING WITH CHERRY SAUCE

YIELD:	8 loaves, 9 oz (300 g) each
PORTIONS:	32
PORTION SIZE:	3½ oz (99 g)

Nutritional Information per Serving		
	Amount	Calories
Calories		194
Fat	6 g	54
Saturated fatty acid	3 g	27
Cholesterol	0 mg	
Carbohydrate	33 g	
Added sugars	NA*	
Fiber	1 g	
Protein	4 g	
Sodium	158 mg	
Potassium	181 mg	
Vitamin A	39 RE	
Vitamin C	1 mg	
Calcium	48 mg	
Iron	2 mg	
* NA = not available.		

	8 oz	Water	225 g	
	2 oz	Cocoa	57 g	
	1 oz	Margarine	28 g	
	2 tsp	Coffee, instant granules	2 g	
	12 oz	Chocolate chips, semisweet	340 g	
	9 oz	Sugar	300 g	
	13 oz	Frozen egg substitute, thawed	365 g	
	8 oz	Pastry flour	220 g	
	6 oz	Whole wheat flour	180 g	
	½ oz	Baking powder	14 g	
	1 tsp	Salt	5 g	
1 lb	1 oz	Skim milk	490 g	
	1 tsp	Vanilla	5 g	
4 lb	12 oz	Total weight	2230 g	

PROCEDURE

1. Combine water, cocoa, margarine, coffee, and chocolate. Cook over low heat until smooth, stirring constantly. Cool completely.

2. Beat sugar and egg substitute at high speed for 5 minutes.

3. Blend in chocolate mixture and beat at low speed 1 minute.

4. Sift flour, baking powder, and salt. Add to chocolate-egg mixture alternately with milk, beating well after each addition.

5. Scale 9½ oz (270 g) batter into each of 8 lightly greased 3¼ × 5¾ in (8 cm × 16 cm) pans.

6. Cover each pan with lightly greased foil. Place in a large shallow pan and add enough boiling water to come halfway up sides of pan.

7. Bake at 275° F (135° C) for 2 hours.

8. Remove pans from water; cool pudding in pan for 15 minutes.

9. Invert puddings. Cut each into four slices.

10. Serve each pudding slice with 1 oz (28 g) sauce.

Cherry Sauce

2 lb	2 oz	Sweet cherries, canned with syrup	960 g
	½ oz	Cornstarch	14 g
	2 oz	Brandy	56 g

1. Drain cherries.
2. Combine juice and cornstarch in a saucepan. Cook over low heat until clear and thickened, stirring constantly.
3. Stir in cherries and brandy.

APRICOT-BANANA MOUSSE

YIELD:	1¾ dozen
PORTIONS:	20
PORTION SIZE:	4 oz (110 g)

2 lb	Bananas, peeled	900 g
1 lb	Apricots, dried	450 g
2 lb	Yogurt, plain, nonfat	900 g
½ oz	Vanilla	14 g
5 lb ½ oz	Total weight	2264 g

PROCEDURE

1. Process all ingredients in a food processor until smooth.

2. Spoon 4 oz (110 g) mousse into each of 20 dessert glasses. Chill several hours before serving.

Nutritional Information per Serving		
	Amount	*Calories*
Calories		118
Fat	<1 g	3
Saturated fatty acid	0 g	
Cholesterol	1 mg	
Carbohydrate	28 g	
Added sugars	0 g	
Fiber	3 g	
Protein	4 g	
Sodium	30 mg	
Potassium	492 mg	
Vitamin A	168 RE	
Vitamin C	5 mg	
Calcium	93 mg	
Iron	1 mg	

RICE PUDDING

YIELD: 9 lb 3 oz (4170 g)
PORTIONS: 36
PORTION SIZE: 4 oz (113 g)

Nutritional Information per Serving		
	Amount	*Calories*
Calories		139
Fat	1 g	9
Saturated fatty acid	<1 g	
Cholesterol	31 mg	
Carbohydrate	30 g	
Added sugars	6 g	
Fiber	1 g	
Protein	4 g	
Sodium	40 mg	
Potassium	192 mg	
Vitamin A	40 RE	
Vitamin C	1 mg	
Calcium	79 mg	
Iron	1 mg	

	2½ oz	Egg yolks	70 g
	9 oz	Egg whites	260 g
	7 oz	Sugar	200 g
1 lb	1 oz	Skim milk, scalded	480 g
	2 tsp	Cinnamon	4 g
	½ tsp	Nutmeg	1 g
	1 oz	Vanilla	28 g
3 lb	4 oz	Skim milk	1470 g
2 lb	12 oz	Rice, long-grain, cooked	1240 g
	15 oz	Raisins	420 g
9 lb	3 oz	Total weight	4170 g

PROCEDURE

1. Beat egg yolks and egg whites on high speed until thick, about 5 minutes.

2. Gradually add sugar and continue mixing 1 minute.

3. Gradually add scalded milk, mixing on low speed until blended.

4. Pour mixture into a large saucepan; cook over medium heat. (Mixture will appear foamy on top.)

5. Cook until temperature reaches 160° F (72° C), stirring constantly with a wire whisk.

6. Remove from heat; stir in spices and vanilla. Set aside. (Mixture will be thick.)

7. Bring remaining milk to a boil over medium heat. Stir frequently.

8. Reduce heat to low; add cooked rice. Cook for 30 minutes or until milk is absorbed. Stir frequently.

9. Fold in egg yolk mixture and raisins.

10. Cool quickly in an ice bath and refrigerate.

GRANNY'S APPLE CRISP

YIELD:	One 12 × 20 in (30 × 50 cm) pan
PORTIONS:	48
PORTION SIZE:	4 oz (113 g)

Nutritional Information per Serving		
	Amount	Calories
Calories		113
Fat	2 g	18
Saturated fatty acid	<1 g	
Cholesterol	<1 mg	
Carbohydrate	23 g	
Added sugars	5 g	
Fiber	2 g	
Protein	2 g	
Sodium	32 mg	
Potassium	184 mg	
Vitamin A	27 RE	
Vitamin C	4 mg	
Calcium	38 mg	
Iron	<1 mg	

Filling

7 lb	8 oz	Granny Smith apples, peeled, sliced	3400 g
	¼ oz	Cinnamon	7 g
	1 tsp	Nutmeg	4 g
	11 oz	Apple juice concentrate, unsweetened, thawed	310 g
	¼ oz	Lemon peel, grated	7 g
8 lb	3 oz	Total weight	3725 g

Topping

	5¾ oz	Oats, regular or quick	163 g
	6 oz	Brown Sugar	170 g
	1¾ oz	Pastry flour	50 g
	3 oz	Margarine	85 g
	4 oz	Apple juice concentrate, unsweetened, thawed	113 g
1 lb	4½ oz	Total weight	580 g

Sauce

	2 oz	Brown sugar	57 g
	¾ oz	Cornstarch	21 g
1 lb	1 oz	Skim milk	490 g
	2 tsp	Rum flavoring	5 g
1 lb	4 oz	Total weight	570 g

PROCEDURE

1. Combine apples, cinnamon, and nutmeg in a large bowl. Toss well. Add apple juice and lemon peel.
2. Spread apples in a 12 × 20 in (30 × 50 cm) pan.
3. Combine oats, sugar, and flour. Add margarine and apple juice and mix until crumbly.
4. Sprinkle topping mixture evenly over apples.
5. Bake at 400° F (200° C), about 25 to 30 minutes or until brown.

SAUCE

1. Combine sugar, cornstarch, and milk. Cook over medium heat until thickened, stirring constantly. Add rum flavoring.
2. Drizzle over warm apple crisp.

GLOSSARY

Adipose tissue Fat tissue.

Amaranth flour Flour milled from the seeds of the amaranth plant, which is a grain native to Central and South America; it is very high in protein.

Amino acid Molecular building block that forms protein.

Anemia Medical condition in which the blood is deficient in red blood cells, hemoglobin, or total volume.

B complex Group of water-soluble vitamins that were originally given the name B, with a subscript number, such as B_1. Today these vitamins have other names; for example, vitamin B_1 is now known as *thiamin*.

Baker's cheese Low-fat cheese made from skim milk; it can be substituted for cream cheese.

Bile Fluid, of which cholesterol is a constituent, secreted by the liver to aid in the digestion of fat.

Bread flour High-protein white flour such as a patent flour, that is used in bread making.

Burrstone Type of rock used to make millstones.

Cake flour Soft, lower-protein flour used for making cakes.

Calcium Mineral that plays an important role in bone and tooth formation.

Calorie Unit of measurement of heat; 1 calorie is equal to the amount of heat needed to raise one gram of water by one Celsius degree. A calorie can thus be used to describe the amount of heat (or energy) given off in the digestion of food. Food Calories (usually written with a capital C) are actually kilocalories.

Canola oil A monousaturated oil made from rapeseed, a small black seed about the size of a mustard seed.

Carbohydrate One of the three essential energy nutrients. Carbohydrates comprise starch, sugar, and fiber, each of which contribute four calories per gram.

Cellulose Indigestible complex carbohydrate that comprises the cell walls of most plants.

Chloride   Negatively charged ion of chlorine; it is found in many places such as table salt (sodium chloride), and in the fluid outside the cells. As an electrolyte, in aids in the control of fluid balance in the body.

Cholesterol   Steroid alcohol (sterol) found only in animal tissues.

Coagulation   Process by which a substance such as blood thickens and clots.

Cocoa   Dry powder produced when cocoa butter is extracted from cocoa paste during the processing of cocoa beans; it contains 12 to 25 percent fat.

Daily Food Guide   USDA publication that recommends servings from each of the four food groups to provide a balanced diet.

Denaturation   Modification of a protein by heat or chemical reaction resulting in a change to the original structure.

Dextrose   Sugar commonly used in baking; it is a form of *glucose* (a monosaccharide).

Diabetic   Term applied to individuals who are unable to properly metabolize carbohydrates. It can also be applied to foods that may have the type or amount of carbohydrates altered.

Dietary fiber   Mostly complex carbohydrate found in plant cell walls that cannot be completely digested by the human digestive system. Examples of dietary fiber include cellulose, pectin, mucilages, and gums.

Dietary Guidelines   Set of seven guidelines modified from the *Dietary Goals for the United States*. The guidelines focus on food recommendations for better health and are based on current research showing the association between diet and health.

Disaccharide   Type of sugar consisting of two monosaccharide molecules; examples include table sugar (sucrose) and malt sugar (maltose).

Emulsifier   Compound that helps one product to stay in suspension with another (for example, the egg yolk binding the oil and water in mayonnaise).

Enriched   Term applied to a refined grain product in which thiamin, riboflavin, niacin, and iron lost in processing have been completely or partially replaced.

Fat-soluble vitamin   One of the four vitamins known to be soluble in fat— vitamins A, D, E, and K.

Flan pan   A round baking pan with a fluted edge and indented center.

Fortification   Practice of adding nutrients to food that do not naturally occur in the food. An example is orange juice with calcium added.

Fructose   Monosaccharide found in fruit and in honey.

Germ   Part of the grain seed containing the plant embryo.

Glucose   Monosaccharide preferred by the human body for energy.

Gluten   Protein in wheat flour that gives elasticity to dough and structure to breads.

Glycogen   Form in which carbohydrates are stored in the body; it is used to provide energy to the muscles.

Graham flour   Stone ground whole wheat flour made from the whole kernel of winter wheat.

Hemoglobin   Spherical protein on red blood cells that carries oxygen.

High-gluten flour   Flour made from hard winter wheat that has a higher protein content, also known as bread flour.

Hydrogenation   Process by which hydrogen ions are attached to molecules of unsaturated fat, thus making the fat more saturated.

Hypoglycemia   Condition characterized by an abnormally low level of sugar in the blood.

Incomplete protein   A protein lacking an essential amino acid.

Lactose   Disaccharide found in milk.

Lecithin   Phospholipid that may act as an emulsifier.

Legume   Plant whose roots contain nitrogen-fixing bacteria. The seed, when dried, has a higher-quality protein than other plants have. Examples include dried beans and peas.

Lipid   Nutrient category containing both solid and liquid fats.

Millstone   Circular stone, used in pairs, between which grains are ground.

Molasses   Thick syrup, varying in color and flavor intensity, produced during the manufacture of sugar.

Monosaccharide   Sugar containing only one saccharide molecule.

Monounsaturated fatty acid   Fatty acid with one double bond.

Neufchatel cheese   Low-fat type of cream cheese with 5 grams of fat per ounce.

Niacin   B vitamin also known as vitamin B_3. It helps release the energy from food.

Noncaloric   Term describing a substance (such as a food) that does not provide calories.

Obese   Term describing a person with excess body fat.

Osteoporosis   Disease whereby bones lose their mineral content with age (the root syllables of the word mean "porous bones").

Pastry flour   Lower-protein white flour used for cookies and pastries.

Pasturized egg products   Frozen or dried whole eggs, egg whites, or egg yolks that have been pasteurized.

Pectin   Type of water-soluble fiber found in fruits.

Phospholipid   Class of lipid containing phosphorus and found in abundance in the body. Such lipids are soluble in both fat and water.

Polysaccharide   Complex carbohydrate made up of several saccharide units. Two examples are starch and fiber.

Polyunsaturated fatty acid   Fatty acid having two or more double bonds.

Potassium   Positively charged ion that is an electrolyte in the body. It is important to the diet because it helps maintain normal blood pressure.

Preservative   Product used to retard food spoilage.

Protein   Energy nutrient providing 4 calories per gram; it is composed of amino acids and is a major component of muscle tissue.

Recommended Dietary Allowances   Publication giving nutritional standards for evaluating the diets of groups and formulating new products, among other information.

Riboflavin   B vitamin also known as vitamin B_2, found predominantly in dairy and grain products.

Ricotta cheese (low-fat)   Ricotta cheese made from skim milk, with a fat content of 1 gram per ounce.

Roller mill   Mill that grinds grain into flour by passing it between a series of high-speed metal rollers.

Rotary hourglass   Large grinding device consisting of two millstones powered by animals or humans.

Saddlestone   Primitive type of grinding tool consisting of a concave bottom stone and an oblong roller stone.

Saturated fatty acid   Fatty acid filled with hydrogen ions. Fats containing large amounts of this are usually solid at room temperature.

Sodium   Positively charged ion that is an electrolyte. It is important to the diet because it may aggravate the condition of high blood pressure.

Soluble   Term describing a substance that can be dissolved.

Sorbitol   Sugar alcohol found in fruits and vegetables and used as a sweetener in some dietetic baked products.

Sour cream (low-fat)   Sour cream made from skim milk, with a fat content of 2 grams per ounce.

Sterol   Steroid alcohol—a class of lipids of which cholesterol is one.

Sucrose   Disaccharide also known as table sugar.

Sulfites   Sulfur-based compounds that act as antioxidants and help preserve the color of certain foods.

Tallow White solid fat rendered from beef.

Thiamin B vitamin that helps the body to release energy from carbohydrates.

Thickener Product that causes a liquid to become thick.

Tofu Product made from soy milk, with the consistency of a soft cheese, very mild flavor, and no cholesterol.

Triglyceride Most abundant fat in plants and animals; it is made up of a glycerol molecule and three fatty acids.

Triticale Grain that is a hybrid of wheat and rye.

Whey Watery part of milk remaining after cheese curd is removed.

Whole-wheat flour Flour milled from the hard wheat kernel, including the bran and germ.

Whole-wheat pastry flour Lower-protein soft flour milled from the entire wheat kernel, including the bran and germ; it is used for cakes and pastries.

HEALTH GUIDE TO FORMULAS

Yeast Breads and Rolls	1	2	3	4	5	6
100% Whole Wheat Bread	x				x	
Herb Bread	x				x	
Oatmeal-Molasses Bread	x					x
Holiday Yeast Bread		x				
Multi-Grain Bread	x				x	
Health Bread	x				x	
Crusty Italian Bread	x				x	
Swedish Rye Bread		x			x	
Dinner Rolls	x					x
Oat Rolls	x					x
Honey-Wheat Rolls	x					x
Raisin Bran Rolls		x				
Cinnamon-Oat Rolls		x				
Crown Rolls in a Ring	x					x
Pecan Rolls						x
Italian Pizza Sticks	x					x
90-Minute Fruit Kuchen	NA			x	x	

Muffins and Quick Breads	1	2	3	4	5	6
Whole Wheat Waffles	x			x		
Grandmother's Hotcakes		x				
Scones	x					x
Buttermilk Biscuits	x				x	

(continued)

Key
1 *Sugar free*—contains less than 5 grams of added sugar
2 *For occasional use*—contains 12 grams or less of added sugar
3 *Very low sodium*—contains 35 mg or less of sodium
4 *Low sodium*—contains 140 mg or less of sodium
5 *Cholesterol free*—contains less than 2 mg of cholesterol
6 *Low cholesterol*—contains less than 20 mg of cholesterol
NA Formula contains prepared ingredients with added sugar. Analytical data on this is not available.

Muffins and Quick Breads (*continued*)	1	2	3	4	5	6
Norwegian Oat Biscuits		x				x
Apple Coffee Cake					x	
Soda Bread	x			x	x	
Strawberry-Nutmeg Bread		x				
Banana Bread		x				x
Date-Nut Bread		x			x	
Cranberry Bread and Muffins		x				x
Raisin Bran Muffins		x				x
Cran-Apple Muffins		x		x	x	
Pumpkin Muffins				x		x
Branana Muffins		x			x	
Lemon-Poppyseed Muffins		x				x
Pineapple-Carrot Muffins		x		x	x	
Double Bran Muffins		x		x		x
Blueberry Muffins		x			x	
Apple-Spice Muffins		x			x	

Cookies and Bars	1	2	3	4	5	6
Jam-Filled Cookies				x	x	
Meringue Kisses		x	x		x	
Icebox Cookies		x		x	x	
Gingersnaps		x		x	x	
Hermits		x		x	x	
Creative Cutout Cookies	x			x		x
Choc-Oat Chip Cookies		x		x		x
Oatmeal-Raisin Cookies		x		x		x
Orange-Molasses Drop Cookies		x		x		x
Strawberry Bars		x		x		x
Sour Cream Brownies				x	x	
Cheesecake Bars		x		x		x
Marble Cheesecake Bars				x		x
Pumpkin Bars		x			x	
Raspberry-Fudge Bars		x		x	x	
Apple Bars				x		x
Fruit Bars	NA			x	x	
Date Bars		x	x		x	

Key
1 *Sugar free*—contains less than 5 grams of added sugar
2 *For occasional use*—contains 12 grams or less of added sugar
3 *Very low sodium*—contains 35 mg or less of sodium
4 *Low sodium*—contains 140 mg or less of sodium
5 *Cholesterol free*—contains less than 2 mg of cholesterol
6 *Low cholesterol*—contains less than 20 mg of cholesterol
NA Formula contains prepared ingredients with added sugar. Analytical data on this is not available.

Cakes	1	2	3	4	5	6
Chocolate-Applesauce Cake				x	x	
Cocoa-Mint Angel Food Cake				x	x	
Gingerbread with Lemon Sauce						x
Pound Cake		x			x	
Prune Cake		x		x	x	
Sponge Cake				x		
Apple Kuchen		x		x	x	
Chocolate Pudding Cake				x	x	
Double Chocolate Cupcakes		x			x	
Pineapple Upside-Down Cake						x
Chocolate Cake with Meringue Icing					x	
Applesauce Picnic Cake				x	x	
Cocoa Chiffon Cake				x		
White Cake				x	x	
Spice Cake					x	
Fruit Flan		x				x
Chocolate-Cherry Torte	NA				x	
Cocoa-Bean Cake		x		x		
Lemon Chiffon Cheesecake				x		
Peanut Squares				x		
Carrot Cake with Creamy Frosting						

Pies and Pastries	1	2	3	4	5	6
Orange Chiffon Pie		x		x	x	
Chocolate Chiffon Pie				x		x
Vanilla (or Chocolate) Cream Pie		x		x		
Pumpkin Pie		x		x	x	
Raspberry (or Strawberry) Cream Pie				x	x	
Crumb-Topped Apple Pie		x		x	x	
Mint-Chocolate Freezer Pie	NA			x		x
Tin Roof Freezer Pie	NA					x
Cherry Freezer Pie	NA					x
Raspberry (or Strawberry) Yogurt Pie		x				x
Strawberry Tartlets	x			x	x	
Fresh Fruit Tart	x			x		x
Banana Orange Tart	x			x	x	

(continued)

Key
1 *Sugar free*—contains less than 5 grams of added sugar
2 *For occasional use*—contains 12 grams or less of added sugar
3 *Very low sodium*—contains 35 mg or less of sodium
4 *Low sodium*—contains 140 mg or less of sodium
5 *Cholesterol free*—contains less than 2 mg of cholesterol
6 *Low cholesterol*—contains less than 20 mg of cholesterol
NA Formula contains prepared ingredients with added sugar. Analytical data on this is not available.

Pies and Pastries (continued)	1	2	3	4	5	6
Pear-Almond Tart	x		x		x	
Eclairs		x		x		
Cherry Turnovers	NA			x		x
Prune Pockets		x		x	x	

Desserts	1	2	3	4	5	6
Apple Snow with Caramel Sauce				x	x	
Almond Cream with Chocolate Sauce				x		x
Peach Cobbler		x		x	x	
Steamed Chocolate Pudding with Cherry Sauce	NA			x		
Apricot-Banana Mousse	x		x		x	
Rice Pudding	x			x		
Granny's Apple Crisp		x	x		x	

Key
1 *Sugar free*—contains less than 5 grams of added sugar
2 *For occasional use*—contains 12 grams or less of added sugar
3 *Very low sodium*—contains 35 mg or less of sodium
4 *Low sodium*—contains 140 mg or less of sodium
5 *Cholesterol free*—contains less than 2 mg of cholesterol
6 *Low cholesterol*—contains less than 20 mg of cholesterol
NA Formula contains prepared ingredients with added sugar. Analytical data on this is not available.

APPENDIX B

RDIs AND DRVs

(Proposed) Reference Daily Intakes (RDIs)* of Selected Vitamins and Minerals
(to replace the U.S. RDAs)

Nutrient	Unit of Measurement	Adults and Children 4 or More Years of Age
Vitamin A	Retinol equivalents (RE)	875
Vitamin C	Milligrams	60
Calcium	Milligrams	900
Iron	Milligrams	12

*From *The Federal Register*, July 19, 1990, pp. 29485–29486.

(Proposed) Daily Reference Values (DRVs)* for substances not included in the 1989 RDAs.

Nutrient	Unit of Measurement	DRV
Fat	Grams	75
Saturated fatty acids	Grams	25
Unsaturated fatty acids	Grams	50
Cholesterol	Milligrams	300
Carbohydrate	Grams	325
Fiber	Grams	25
Sodium	Milligrams	2400
Potassium	Milligrams	3500

*From *The Federal Register*, July 19, 1990, pp. 29485–29486.

INDEX